READINGS ON

E. SCOTT
FITZGERALD

THE GREENHAVEN PRESS

Literary Companion

TO AMERICAN AUTHORS

READINGS ON

F. SCOTT FITZGERALD

David Bender, *Publisher*

Bruno Leone, *Executive Editor*

Brenda Stalcup, *Managing Editor*

Bonnie Szumski, *Series Editor*

Katie de Koster, *Book Editor*

Library of Congress Cataloging-in-Publication Data

Readings on F. Scott Fitzgerald / Katie de Koster, book editor.
        p.   cm. — (Greenhaven Press literary companion
to American authors)
        ISBN 1-56510-460-9 (pbk. : alk. paper). —
ISBN 1-56510-461-7 (lib. : alk. paper)
        1. Fitzgerald, F. Scott (Frances Scott), 1896–1940—Crit-
icism and interpretation. I. de Koster, Katie, 1948-   . II.
Series.
PS3511.I9Z8   1998
813'.52—dc20
                                                96-44977
                                                    CIP

Every effort has been made to trace the owners of copy-
righted material. The articles in this volume may have
been edited for content, length, and/or reading level. The
titles have been changed to enhance the editorial purpose
of the Opposing Viewpoints® concept. Those interested in
locating the original source will find the complete citation
on the first page of each article.

Cover photo: The Bettmann Archive; pages 14 and 24, Library of Congress; page 28, National Archives

Copyright ©1998 by Greenhaven Press, Inc.
PO Box 289009
San Diego, CA 92198-9009
Printed in the U.S.A.

"Mostly, we authors must repeat ourselves—that's the truth. We have two or three great and moving experiences in our lives—experiences so great and moving that it doesn't seem at the time that anyone else has been so caught up and pounded and dazzled and astonished and beaten and broken and rescued and illuminated and rewarded and humbled in just that way before.

Then we learn our trade, well or less well, and we tell our two or three stories—each time in a new disguise—maybe ten times, maybe a hundred, as long as people will listen."

F. Scott Fitzgerald,
"One Hundred False Starts"

CONTENTS

Chapter 1: Fitzgerald as the Living Symbol of His Time

Chapter 2: *The Great Gatsby*

Chapter 3: *Tender Is the Night*

FOREWORD

"'Tis the good reader that
makes the good book."

Ralph Waldo Emerson

The story's bare facts are simple: The captain, an old and scarred seafarer, walks with a peg leg made of whale ivory. He relentlessly drives his crew to hunt the world's oceans for the great white whale that crippled him. After a long search, the ship encounters the whale and a fierce battle ensues. Finally the captain drives his harpoon into the whale, but the harpoon line catches the captain about the neck and drags him to his death.

A simple story, a straightforward plot—yet, since the 1851 publication of Herman Melville's *Moby-Dick*, readers and critics have found many meanings in the struggle between Captain Ahab and the whale. To some, the novel is a cautionary tale that depicts how Ahab's obsession with revenge leads to his insanity and death. Others believe that the whale represents the unknowable secrets of the universe and that Ahab is a tragic hero who dares to challenge fate by attempting to discover this knowledge. Perhaps Melville intended Ahab as a criticism of Americans' tendency to become involved in well-intentioned but irrational causes. Or did Melville model Ahab after himself, letting his fictional character express his anger at what he perceived as a cruel and distant god?

Although literary critics disagree over the meaning of *Moby-Dick*, readers do not need to choose one particular interpretation in order to gain an understanding of Melville's novel. Instead, by examining various analyses, they can gain numerous insights into the issues that lie under the surface of the basic plot. Studying the writings of literary critics can also aid readers in making their own assessments of *Moby-Dick* and other literary works and in developing analytical thinking skills.

The Greenhaven Literary Companion Series was created with these goals in mind. Designed for young adults, this unique anthology series provides an engaging and comprehensive introduction to literary analysis and criticism. The essays included in the Literary Companion Series are chosen for their accessibility to a young adult audience and are expertly edited in consideration of both the reading and comprehension levels of this audience. In addition, each essay is introduced by a concise summation that presents the contributing writer's main themes and insights. Every anthology in the Literary Companion Series contains a varied selection of critical essays that cover a wide time span and express diverse views. Wherever possible, primary sources are represented through excerpts from authors' notebooks, letters, and journals and through contemporary criticism.

Each title in the Literary Companion Series pays careful consideration to the historical context of the particular author or literary work. In-depth biographies and detailed chronologies reveal important aspects of authors' lives and emphasize the historical events and social milieu that influenced their writings. To facilitate further research, every anthology includes primary and secondary source bibliographies of articles and/or books selected for their suitability for young adults. These engaging features make the Greenhaven Literary Companion series ideal for introducing students to literary analysis in the classroom or as a library resource for young adults researching the world's great authors and literature.

Exceptional in its focus on young adults, the Greenhaven Literary Companion Series strives to present literary criticism in a compelling and accessible format. Every title in the series is intended to spark readers' interest in leading American and world authors, to help them broaden their understanding of literature, and to encourage them to formulate their own analyses of the literary works that they read. It is the editors' hope that young adult readers will find these anthologies to be true companions in their study of literature.

INTRODUCTION

Daedalus was the legendary Athenian who built the Minotaur's maze for Minos, the king of Crete, and then built wings of wax and feathers for himself and his son Icarus so that they could escape the island. He warned his son not to fly too close to the sun, then watched helplessly as Icarus, delighting in the freedom of flying, soared so high that his wings melted and he plunged into the Aegean Sea.

America in the 1920s was much like Icarus.

The Roaring Twenties. Prohibition. The Great Crash. During the distinctive, wild period between two world wars (especially during the singular decade of the 1920s), American author F. Scott Fitzgerald wrote and lived a life that reflected the great soaring ride—and eventual crash—his country was taking. An amazingly precise observer and chronicler, Fitzgerald preserved his world in words that draw the reader immediately into the swirl of changes America was experiencing and make that time as vivid as today's news.

Arthur Wrobel of the University of Kentucky cites

> Fitzgerald's receptiveness to and assimilation of the whole range of his world's cultural matrix—from popular to elite—from T.S. Eliot's *The Waste Land* and Joseph Conrad's *Heart of Darkness* to Warner Fabian's *Flaming Youth,* articles that appeared in *Photoplay* and the blues lyrics of W.C. Handy. Fitzgerald's insights about his age, we discover, are coincident with observations made by George Santayana in *Character and Opinion in the United States,* Walter Lippmann in his newspaper columns, Robert S. Lynd and Helen Merrell Lynd in *Middletown,* and Emily Post in *Etiquette.*

Fitzgerald's short stories and novels are great entertainment. But he also repays the attentive reader with an understanding of that boisterous, chaotic period in American history, as well as with an early challenge to the idea and ideals of the American Dream—before that term had even been coined.

Fitzgerald exposes the recklessness of the Twenties, the excesses, intemperance, and dissipation that followed both the end of World War I and the passage of Prohibition (the

Eighteenth Amendment to the Constitution unsuccessfully banned alcoholic beverages from 1919 to 1933). He especially loved to provoke and perturb his elders by writing about the naughty habits of his peers; like many of his generation, he and his characters rejected not just their parents' life choices but many of their deepest values. And after writing stories centered on college kids (just after he left college) and stories of young adults burning their candles not just at both ends but all along their length (as he was doing), he invented characters—Jay Gatsby, Dick Diver—who crashed when they (like himself) could not sustain the intense passions of their lives.

At the end of the Roaring Twenties, America—like Icarus, like Jay Gatsby and Dick Diver, like Scott Fitzgerald—crashed: On October 29, 1929, the stock market collapsed and the Great Depression began. The wild ride was over for both the country and Fitzgerald, whose work lost its appeal to people struggling with economic disaster. It was left to later generations to rediscover the author whose work brings alive the nervous glitter of one of America's gaudiest decades.

The Greenhaven Press Literary Companion to F. Scott Fitzgerald, like each book in the series, also includes a biography of the author that helps illuminate the connections and cross-fertilization between life and work; a chronology that combines the major events in the author's life and concurrent major events in history; a listing of the author's works; and a gateway to further research, in this case through both other books and the internet.

F. Scott Fitzgerald: A Biography

"There never was a good biography of a novelist. There couldn't be. He is too many people, if he's any good."

—F. Scott Fitzgerald

F. Scott Fitzgerald gave the Jazz Age its name when he titled his second collection of short stories *Tales of the Jazz Age.* He wrote the novel that to many people epitomizes the era, *The Great Gatsby.* And, for a brief decade, he and his wife, Zelda, lived the life most people think of when they hear "the Jazz Age." Yet, although Fitzgerald rode the crest of the wave of his times, his early life hardly suggested his later popularity.

An Unsettled Childhood

Francis Scott Key Fitzgerald was born September 24, 1896, in St. Paul, Minnesota, to Edward and Mary McQuillan Fitzgerald. He was named for a distant relative of his father, Francis Scott Key, writer of the poem later set to music as "The Star-Spangled Banner." Edward's heritage was English, his background the genteel southern grace of Maryland. Fitzgerald biographer Jeffrey Meyers says he was "a small, ineffectual man with well-cut clothes and fine Southern manners." His legacy to his only son was in part a sense of gentility and southern standards of gentlemanly behavior. To Scott, Edward seemed a man in the wrong time, an eighteenth-century soul who lived into the twentieth century: "He was of the generation of the colony and the revolution." His memories of helping Confederate snipers and spies enlivened his son's early years and gave him a taste both for adventure and for a well-told tale.

Mary ("Mollie") McQuillan, Scott's mother, came from Irish stock; her grandparents had come to America to escape desperate poverty in Ireland. They were not genteel, but they were financially successful, which Edward was not. Mollie was never conventionally pretty (her husband said, with southern gallantry, that she "just missed being beautiful"), and after financial reverses left the Fitzgeralds dependent on her father's legacy, Mollie abandoned the attempt to keep up her personal appearance (neglecting both grooming and fashion), which embarrassed her fastidious son. Scott later recorded a dream in which he admitted being ashamed of her because she was not young (she was thirty when she married) and elegant. In "An Author's

Remembering his youth, Fitzgerald said: "That was always my experience—a poor boy in a rich town; a poor boy in a rich boy's school; a poor boy in a rich man's club at Princeton. . . . I have never been able to forgive the rich for being rich, and it has colored my entire life and works."

Mother" he described her as "a halting old lady in a black silk dress and a rather preposterously high-crowned hat that some milliner had foisted upon her declining sight." According to Jeffrey Meyers:

> A voracious but indiscriminate reader of sentimental poetry and popular fiction, she was often seen carrying piles of books from the local library. She toted an umbrella even in fine weather and wore mismatched shoes of different colors [she liked to break in a new pair of shoes "one at a time"]. Mollie was also accustomed to blurting out embarrassingly frank remarks without realizing their effect on her acquaintances. She once stared at a woman whose husband was dying and said: "I'm trying to decide how you'll look in mourning."

Scott was his parents' third child, but his two older sisters, ages one and three, died during this pregnancy. Having lost two children (another, born four years later, lived only an hour), Mollie coddled her son, worrying constantly about his health and catering to his whims. Oddly, her attempts to spoil him strengthened his distaste for her. In what most biographers consider an autobiographical passage in *Tender Is the Night*, he wrote that the hero "was born several months after the death of two young sisters and his father, guessing what would be the effect on Dick's mother, had saved him from a spoiling by becoming his moral guide." Yet, as Scott wrote later to his daughter, Scottie, the spoiling had its ill effects: "I didn't know till 15 that there was anyone in the world except me, and it cost me *plenty.*"

Edward headed a firm called the American Rattan and Willow Works, which produced wicker furniture in St. Paul; the business failed in 1898. In April of that year the Fitzgeralds moved to Buffalo, New York, where Edward became a soap salesman for Proctor and Gamble. They stayed there for most of the next ten years, except for a temporary move to Syracuse from January 1901 to September 1903, where Scott's only sibling, Annabel, was born in July 1901. Back in Buffalo in time for his seventh birthday, Scott invited his old friends to his birthday party. It rained, and no one came. (His mother allowed him to eat the entire birthday cake—candles included—as consolation.)

In March 1908, Edward Fitzgerald lost his job with Proctor and Gamble. Scott recalled, "That morning he had gone out a comparatively young man, a man full of strength, full of confidence. He came home that evening, an old man, a completely broken man. He had lost his essential drive, his immaculateness of purpose. He was a failure the rest of his days." Mollie retreated into hysteria, and frequently remarked to Scott that the family would be lost but for support from the McQuillans. The force of this blow is echoed in Jeffrey Meyers's judgment that "Fitzgerald inherited his elegance and propensity to failure from his father, his social insecurity and absurd behavior from his mother."

Returning to St. Paul in defeat, Edward took up the McQuillan trade of wholesale grocery sales, working from a desk in his brother-in-law's real estate office. For several months the children lived with their grandmother McQuillan while Edward and Mollie moved in with a friend. But the move did have its bright side: In New York, the family had changed residences nearly every year, so the children had developed no long-term friendships. In St. Paul, although the family continued to move often, they stayed in the same general neighborhood. With McQuillan backing, they had a place in society, and with McQuillan money, they managed to attend the right schools and maintain a respectable social status.

A Writer, Not a Scholar

Scott had always been an excellent storyteller; at the age of five he had startled relatives with a tale of "his" pony so full of details that afterward it was hard to convince them it was all a fantasy. On the other hand, he had always been an indulged and indifferent scholar. When he first went off to school, he made such a fuss that he was told he need only attend half a day—which half was up to him. By the time he entered St. Paul Academy at the age of twelve, Scott had launched himself into a literary career at the expense of his other studies. "I wrote all through every class in school in the back of my geography book and first year Latin and on the margins of themes and declensions and mathematics problems," he later recalled. In addition to adventure stories for the school newspaper, he penned melodramatic plays for the Elizabethan Dramatic Club (named not for the queen of Shakespeare's time but for the club's founder, Elizabeth Magoffin).

His poor academic performance disappointed his parents, who hoped a strict boarding school would help. Scott eagerly set off for the Newman School in Hackensack, New Jersey, believing that his attractive appearance, social graces, and intelligence would make him popular. He was sadly disappointed; this was when he learned, as he later wrote to Scottie, that the world did not revolve around him. Although he tried to curry favor with his classmates by writing their English papers for them, the strategy won him no permanent friends. Fitzgerald biographer Arthur Mizener quotes his roommate, Martin Amorous, as saying Scott had "the most impenetrable egotism I've ever seen"; yet Scott was constantly aware, Amorous added, that "he was one of the poorest boys in a rich boys' school."

From Newman and his lack of social success, Scott frequently escaped across the Hudson River into New York to attend the theater. His new ambition was to write musical comedy as successful as that of Gilbert and Sullivan, whose works he studied with a devotion that would have delighted his teachers had he applied it to his schoolwork.

Still academically indifferent, Scott was receiving encouragement for his creative efforts. During the summers, when he was home from Newman, the Elizabethan Dramatic Club performed his plays, turning a small profit for the charitable causes it benefited. And while he was at Newman he developed a strong rapport with a worldly priest who was a school trustee, Father Sigourney Webster Fay. Father Fay, who frequently invited Scott to his Washington home, encouraged Scott to develop his talent and introduced him to his friends among the intellectual and social elite, including writer and historian Henry Adams and the wealthy and well-connected Shane Leslie, who later recommended Scott's first novel to Scribner's and wrote a favorable review of it.

Such encouragement notwithstanding, Scott's academic performance continued to suffer, and when he decided to attend Princeton University, he was told that his grades were inadequate for admission. He took an entrance exam, failed it, spent the summer studying, then went to New Jersey to take the makeup entrance exam—and again failed to make the grade. It says something for his powers of persuasiveness that he managed to talk the school authorities into granting him a probationary acceptance.

PRINCETON

Sergio Perosa, in *The Art of F. Scott Fitzgerald*, describes Fitzgerald's adjustments to the "rich and unprejudiced" East after having been raised in the "closed and conservative" Middle West.

These years at Princeton were the most intense and determinant phase of Fitzgerald's development. They were years of exultation and depression, of intellectual awakening, as well as of misdirected energy. His athletic ambitions were shattered, he suffered repeated humiliations from companions richer than he; but at Princeton he found his way to literary achievement. Quickly, after an initial moment of ostracism, Fitzgerald became a member of the Triangle Club and of the editorial board of the *Daily Princetonian,* contributed to the *Nassau Lit.* and *The Tiger,* and was admitted to one of the best eating clubs. There is something impressive in the lucid perception with which the young outsider discovered the subtle secrets of the place, and in the iron will with which he pursued his social and cultural aims under a pretense of aristocratic detachment.

Although Scott was once again a poor boy in a rich man's environment, he did make some lifelong friends. John Peale Bishop and Edmund ("Bunny") Wilson both made literary names for themselves, and both helped Scott develop and find his focus as a writer. Their opinions of his works were important to him for the rest of his life.

THE TRIANGLE CLUB

The Triangle Club wrote, composed, and produced musical comedies; during Christmas vacations the club presented their productions at college campuses across the country. Not surprisingly, this is where Scott's energies were focused, again at the expense of his academic studies. When one of his professors protested his frequent tardiness, he exclaimed, "Sir—it's absurd to expect me to be on time. I'm a genius!"

Genius or no, failing grades could keep Scott from fulfilling his campus ambitions. He later recalled, "I spent my entire freshman year writing an operetta for the Triangle Club. I failed in algebra, trigonometry, coordinate geometry and hygiene, but the Triangle Club accepted my show, and by tutoring all through a stuffy August I managed to come back a sophomore and act in it as a chorus girl." And a stunningly beautiful showgirl he was, too. Although he was forbidden to travel with the company during the Christmas break because of his poor grades, his photograph as a sexy chorine appeared in newspapers in all the towns where the company toured.

In St. Paul instead of on the road at Christmas during his sophomore year, Scott met Ginevra King and fell in love. The sophisticated, sixteen-year-old King came from Lake Forest, "a suburb which epitomized the zenith of upper-class Midwestern society," according to Jeffrey Meyers. Fitzgerald scholar Matthew J. Bruccoli notes that Ginevra "matched his dreams of the perfect girl: beautiful, rich, socially secure, and sought after. The last qualification was important. His ideal girl had to be one pursued by many men; there had to be an element of competition."

Scott's two-year pursuit of Ginevra gave him literary material rather than romantic satisfaction (she provided the model for the heroine, Rosalind, in *This Side of Paradise,* as well as for women in other stories). That she was not impressed with his potential future may be judged by the fact that in 1917 she destroyed the hundreds of letters he had sent her. Although he had begun to feel the relationship was doomed in 1916 when he overheard someone say that "poor boys should not think of marrying rich girls," he kept her letters for many years after they broke up.

One of Ginevra's first literary appearances, according to most scholars, was as the female lead in a story Fitzgerald wrote for the *Nassau Lit.*, Princeton's literary magazine. Matthew Bruccoli describes "The Pierian Springs and the Last Straw":

> The story develops a major theme in Fitzgerald's fiction: the gifted man ruined by a selfish woman. The hero is a scandalous middle-aged novelist who lost his Ginevra as a young man and never got over it. When he marries her after she is widowed, he stops writing. Much of Fitzgerald's fiction would take the form of self-warnings or self-judgments, and this story is the first in which he analyzed the conflicting pulls of love and literature. The girl is the writer's inspiration, but only when she is unattained. The satisfied artist is unproductive.

THINGS FALL APART

By 1917 his romance with Ginevra was not the only thing falling apart. While the Triangle Club was the second-most important organization on campus (after the football team), success there did not impress the academic authorities. During his entire Princeton career, Fitzgerald struggled with makeup studies while failing current courses. Finally, on the verge of failing completely, he contracted malaria (a common ailment then on the marshy campus) and chose to leave "because of illness" during November of his junior year (which he was repeating). He had hoped to become president of the Triangle Club, and the dashing of that hope was a bitterness he carried for the rest of his life. It seemed unreasonable to him that the university should fail to recognize and make allowances for an artist—specifically, for him. Once again, he turned his disappointment into grist for his literary mill. Arthur Mizener writes:

> It puzzled and angered him to find that important things like the Triangle Club and his career as a Big Man could be interfered with by the academic authorities and he was presently to write a story about this experience of taking make-up examinations called "The Spire and the Gargoyle," in which the Spire is the imitation Gothic architecture of Princeton which stands for all the romantic success Fitzgerald dreamed of and the Gargoyle the instructor who graded his make-up examination. The irony of the story depends on the absurdity of a superior and more sensitive person like Fitzgerald's finding himself at the mercy of this pathetic worm. This is the perennial undergraduate attitude, of course, but Fitzgerald's version of it has a kind of classic perfection.

The scars of his rejection were still with him twenty years later, when he recalled: "To me, college would never be the same. There were to be no badges of pride, no medals, after all. It seemed on one . . . afternoon I had lost every single thing I wanted." And when the president of Princeton wrote him objecting mildly to the impression in *This Side of Paradise* that "our young men are merely living for four years in a country club and spending their lives wholly in a spirit of calculation and snobbery," Fitzgerald responded that the book was

> written with the bitterness of my discovery that I had spent several years trying to fit in with a curriculum that is after all made for the average student. After the curriculum had tied me up, taken away the honors I'd wanted, bent my nose over a chemistry book and said, "No fun, no activities, no offices, no Triangle trips—no, not even a diploma if you can't do chemistry"—after that I retired.

THE GREAT WAR

In Europe, the conflict that would come to be known as the First World War had begun in 1914. Although the United States did not officially enter the fighting until 1917, several of Fitzgerald's Princeton classmates had volunteered to fight and some had already died overseas. In July 1917 Fitzgerald took the examinations for a provisional appointment as a second lieutenant in the regular army (he could not become an officer until he reached twenty-one in September), and he received his commission that October. He immediately went to Brooks Brothers in New York to order tailored uniforms and then wrote his mother, warning her not to indulge in dramatics:

> About the army please let's not have either tragedy or Hero-ics because they are equally distasteful to me. I went into this perfectly cold bloodedly and don't sympathize with the "Give my son to country" . . . or "Hero stuff" . . . because *I just went* and purely for *social reasons.* If you want to pray, pray for my soul and not that I won't get killed—the last doesn't seem to matter particularly and if you are a good Catholic the first ought to.

> To a profound pessimist about life, being in danger is not de-pressing. I have never been more cheerful.

Fitzgerald trained at various locations around the country for the next few months. At Fort Leavenworth, Kansas, lead-ing the provisional officers in calisthenics and bayonet drills was a young, blue-eyed captain named Dwight David Eisen-hower, who would follow his success as a general in the *next* world war with a two-term stint as president of the United States. Fitzgerald was not much interested in drills, though; once again, his studies were ignored as he scribbled through his classes and hid his writing pad behind his copy of *Small Problems for Infantry* (apparently unaware of the fact that lives would depend on his military knowledge were he to lead men into battle). He was working on "The Romantic Egoist" (which would eventually be published as *This Side of Paradise*), rushing to finish it and find a publisher before he went off to war, where he was sure he would be killed. After he was caught writing during evening study periods, he shifted to spending his entire weekend writing: "I wrote a one hundred and twenty thousand word novel on the con-secutive weekends of three months," he reported.

Writing was somewhat complicated by frequent transfers around the country; by March 1918 he was at Camp Zachary Taylor, near Louisville, Kentucky; in April he was in Augusta, Georgia, at Camp Gordon; in June he became part of the Ninth Division at Camp Sheridan, near Montgomery, Al-abama. His regiment was just about to leave for France—it had even boarded the ship, then disembarked—when the war ended on November 11, 1918. Although he regretted for the rest of his life that "I Never Got Over" (as he titled a later short story), the men who might have fought under him were probably fortunate. He had already seriously endangered another company when he mistakenly ordered his men to fire on it; he went to visit Princeton when he was supposed to be supervising the unloading of equipment in Hoboken, New Jersey, and thousands of dollars' worth of matériel was stolen; and, although his companions generally liked him, one who served with him during most of his military "career," Alonzo Myers, gently phrased the prevailing opinion: "As an Army officer, Fitzgerald was unusually dispensable."

ZELDA

From June 1918 to February 1919, Scott spent most of his time stationed in Montgomery, Alabama. It was there in July 1918 that he met Zelda Sayre, daughter of a prominent though not wealthy family (her father was an associate justice of the Alabama Supreme Court). Zelda had just graduated from high school and turned eighteen the month they met. According to Jeffrey Meyers, "Protected by the respectability and prestige of her family, Zelda was known for her striking beauty, her unconventional behavior and her sexual promiscuity." (Some biographers believe her flirtations did not lead to sexual activity, suggesting more than was delivered.) Virginia Foster Durr, who knew her in Montgomery, told Meyers:

> Zelda was like a vision of beauty dancing by. She was funny, amusing, the most popular girl, envied by all the others, worshipped and adored, besieged by all the boys. She *did* try to shock. At a dance she pinned mistletoe on the back of her skirt, as if to challenge the young men to kiss her bottom.
>
> In the South women were not supposed to *do* anything. It was sufficient to be beautiful and charming. Zelda, a spoiled baby just out of high school, never even learned to read or sew. She was always treated like a visiting film star: radiant, glowing, desired by all. Since she had absolutely nothing to do and no personal resources to draw on, she later bothered Scott when he was trying to write. She had no ability to suffer adversity, and was unprepared for it when it came.

When Scott first saw Zelda, she was surrounded by young men—with an army base nearby, she had plenty of admirers. The spirit of competition kicked in, and Scott became determined to win her for himself. Throughout their lives together, the admiration of other men for Zelda would both gratify and torment Scott: gratify, because she married him; torment, because she continued to respond to other men to make him jealous.

Unlike Ginevra King, Zelda wanted something Scott could provide: an escape from the provincial life of an Alabama town. By the time he was discharged from his unit in February 1919 (so dispensable, he was one of the first of his unit to be let go), he thought he might join his friend Edmund Wilson, who was leading a comfortable life in the literary circle of New York. He would soon, he hoped, be settled in a lucrative and congenial position and be able to afford to marry and have a cozy apartment, like Wilson's, in Greenwich Village in Manhattan.

Instead he found work writing advertising slogans for signs on streetcars. He moved into a dingy, depressing room far uptown, which he decorated with the rejection slips he received for the stories and sketches he was unable to sell. He visited Zelda in Montgomery three times in the spring of 1919 and tried to persuade her to marry him. Although she professed her love for him, she refused to consider marriage until he was better able to support a wife. Her family also objected, feeling, as Meyers puts it, "that she needed a strong, reliable husband who could control rather than encourage her wild behavior. In their view, he was an unstable Irish Catholic who had not graduated from college, had no career and drank too much."

Impatient with his failures, Zelda broke off their engagement that June. Although she would agree to marry Scott when *This Side of Paradise* was published, the fact that she would not marry him before he had proved himself, and was even willing to give him up if he did not, took much of the sparkle out of the relationship for Scott once it resumed. Then again, perhaps the sparkle could not have survived anyway: Once Zelda said yes, she was no longer the unattainable ideal he had found in Ginevra King.

Scott and Zelda looked enough alike to be taken for brother and sister, and they seemed to bring out a wild need in each other to run amok. Although there were good times, it was to prove an odd, twisted relationship that eventually led, inexorably it seemed, to Zelda's schizophrenia. In the end they were unable to live together, but they never divorced.

PUBLICATION

Just as the war he never got to led him to Zelda, Zelda's refusal to marry him led Scott back to writing. He quit his job in New York and returned to St. Paul, where he devoted himself to work on *This Side of Paradise.* Maxwell Perkins, a young editor at Scribner's, had responded encouragingly to the first draft and suggested improvements. Scott finished the second draft in early September 1919 and shipped it off to Perkins. With a speed unheard-of today, especially for a first novel, Perkins wrote Scott on September 16: "I am very glad, personally, to be able to write to you that we are all for publishing your book, *This Side of Paradise.* . . . It abounds in energy and life. . . . The book is so different that it is hard to prophesy how it will sell but we are all for taking a chance and supporting it with vigor."

Scott was so excited that he ran up and down the street, stopping friends and strangers alike to tell them of his good fortune. Then he returned to New York to accept what he expected would be the accolades of an adoring world.

That summer he seemed to have found the key to his power as a professional writer. Now his stories began to sell, too. Not only did his first story in a mass circulation magazine ("Head and Shoulders," published in the February 1920 *Saturday Evening Post*) earn $400 for the serial (magazine) rights, but he sold the movie rights for the very generous sum of $2,500. Now he was a success; now Zelda would marry him. *This Side of Paradise* came out on March 26, 1920; Scott and Zelda were married on April 3. A year later,

Scott and Zelda on their honeymoon. Their lives took a dramatic turn in the spring of 1920: *This Side of Paradise* was published on March 26; they were married on April 3.

Zelda was pregnant; their only child, Frances Scott ("Scottie") Fitzgerald, was born on October 26, 1921.

ACCLAIM

On one hand, it was naïve for Fitzgerald to expect fame and fortune to follow the publication of a first novel. On the other hand, that's what happened. Burton Rascoe wrote in the *Chicago Daily Tribune* (dated on Scott's wedding day):

> If you have not already done so, make a note of the name, F. Scott Fitzgerald. It is borne by a 23-year-old novelist who will, unless I am much mistaken, be much heard of hereafter. His first novel *This Side of Paradise* gives him, I think, a fair claim to membership in that small squad of contemporary American fictionists who are producing literature. It is sincere, it is honest, it is intelligent, it is handled in an individual manner, it bears the impress, it seems to me, of genius. It is the only adequate study that we have had of the contemporary American in adolescence and young manhood. . . .
>
> It is a novel which is, curiously, important largely through its apparent defects—its bland egotism, its conceited extravagance, its immaturity of thoughts. The hero is frequently a prig, a snob, an ass, and—may I whisper it?—something of a cad; but a youth is all these things.

The *New York Times* raved, "The glorious spirit of abounding youth glows throughout this fascinating tale." The influential H.L. Mencken wrote in the *Smart Set,* "In *This Side of Paradise* [Fitzgerald] offers a truly amazing first novel—original in structure, extremely sophisticated in manner, and adorned with a brilliancy that is as rare in American writing as honesty is in American statecraft." The London *Times Literary Supplement* was more judicious in its response, finding the novel "tiresome" but of interest "as evidence of the intellectual and moral reaction that has set in among the more advanced American circles."

And how should a genius, who months before had briefly taken a job repairing train roofs in Minnesota, deal with such praise? The Fitzgerald of 1932 looked back at the Fitzgerald who had fled the city in 1919 and recalled:

> When I returned six months later the offices of editors and publishers were open to me, impresarios begged plays, the movies panted for screen material. To my bewilderment, I was adopted, not as a Middle Westerner, not even as a detached observer, but as the arch type of what New York wanted. . . .
>
> For just a moment, the "younger generation" idea became a fusion of many elements in New York life. . . . The blending of the bright, gay, vigorous elements began then and for the first

time there appeared a society a little livelier than the solid mahogany dinner parties of Emily Price Post. . . . For the first time an educated European could envisage a trip to New York as something more amusing than a gold-trek into a formalized Australian Bush.

For just a moment, before it was demonstrated that I was unable to play the role, I, who knew less of New York than any reporter of six months standing and less of its society than any hall-room boy in a Ritz stag line, was pushed into the position not only of spokesman for the time but of the typical product of that same moment. I, or rather it was "we" now, did not know exactly what New York expected of us and found it rather confusing. Within a few months after our embarkation on the Metropolitan venture we scarcely knew any more who we were and we hadn't a notion what we were. A dive into a civic fountain, a casual brush with the law, was enough to get us into the gossip columns, and we were quoted on a variety of subjects we knew nothing about. . . . We felt like small children in a great bright unexplored barn. . . .

It was typical of our precarious position in New York that when our child was to be born we played safe and went home to St. Paul. . . . But in a year we were back and we began doing the same things over again and not liking them so much. . . . By this time we "knew everybody." . . .

But we were no longer important. The flapper, upon whose activities the popularity of my first books was based, had become *passé* by 1923.

The flapper may have become passé among New York sophisticates, but Fitzgerald's star was still ascendant. It was a time when short stories were widely and eagerly read, and the short story market was lucrative. In fact, until the last few years of his life, short stories supported Scott and Zelda in the style to which they wished to become accustomed; he earned more for them than he did from books, and he could whip them out much more easily than novels (which he considered his true work) whenever the coffers were empty. Fitzgerald published a book of short stories after each novel; the one that followed *This Side of Paradise* was *Flappers and Philosophers.* His next novel, *The Beautiful and Damned,* was published in April 1922; that September, *Tales of the Jazz Age* established Fitzgerald as proprietor of the name of the era. By then the Fitzgeralds were living on Long Island, New York; they were there when Scott's play *The Vegetable* closed during out-of-town tryouts, a blow that put a disturbing cramp in their enjoyment of celebrity.

By now the frantic pace of their lives was becoming less fun and more destructive: Scott would disappear on three-day benders, finally showing up asleep on the front lawn; they spent money as if it were a challenge; their New York friends were, Scott said, turning their home into "a roadhouse." In May 1924 they set sail for Europe. Scott said they would stay away until he had accomplished some great thing.

For the next two and a half years, the Fitzgeralds spent most of their time in Paris or on the Riviera. Unlike most of their contemporary expatriates, Scott did not attempt to immerse himself in the culture of Europe. Fitzgerald biographer Andrew Turnbull reports:

> For the most part he was indifferent to the foreign culture which the rest of the group were doing their best to absorb. [Poet Archibald] MacLeish, for example, would get Italians to read Cavalconti in the original, so he could savor the rhythms. That was not Fitzgerald's approach at all. His tastes were incorrigibly American, and when offered the English "Abdullah" cigarettes that many of his friends were smoking, he would apologize with a sort of pride for being a Midwesterner who preferred Chesterfields. He made no effort to improve his stumbling French, nor did he concern himself with French art, architecture, or theater. . . . Most Europeans considered him a sensitive boor, without real cultivation or finesse. He used to infuriate the waiters at the casino by praising the German military, saying such things as, "Those Germans are going to come through here some day and wipe you up."

While Ernest Hemingway, for example, was in Europe turning his experiences there into *The Sun Also Rises* (1926), Fitzgerald had, as he had said he would, carried the atmosphere of Long Island with him to Europe. Away from the United States, Scott wrote the very American *Great Gatsby,* accomplishing the "great thing" he had promised.

CRACKS IN THE GLITTERING FACADE

While Fitzgerald was working on *Gatsby,* Zelda had a brief flirtation with a dashing young aviator, Edouard Jozan. Although she had always been flirtatious—her biographer Nancy Milford writes of her "necking with young men because she liked the shapes of their noses or the cut of their dinner jackets"—this seemed more serious. According to Milford, Fitzgerald later reported that Zelda had asked for a divorce so that she could marry Jozan. Scott objected, Zelda gave in, and Jozan left town. Many biographers believe that this affair left a permanent crack in the Fitzgeralds' relationship, although they continued to love each other until they died.

Zelda seemed to enjoy living dangerously; friends noted, for example, that when she was driving she liked to turn to Scott at a particularly dangerous spot on the road and ask him to light her cigarette. Dorothy Parker remembered their first meeting: Zelda was riding the hood of a taxi (with Scott perched on the roof). But it was around this time that Zelda took an overdose of sleeping pills, one of several unsuccessful attempts to take her own life. Many people found Scott and Zelda incredibly attractive and charming, but those who spent time with Zelda often remarked that she

Scott, Zelda, and their daughter, Scottie. Scott's letters to his daughter were full of advice on such topics as how to talk to boys and how to write. He once wrote her: "All good writing is swimming under water and holding your breath."

seemed frantic, desperate, and strange. She would become more so over the years, until her actions were no longer simply the outrageous antics of a flapper but the uncontrollable behavior of a mentally ill woman. In time, Zelda would be diagnosed as incurably schizophrenic.

FITZGERALD AND HEMINGWAY

Gatsby was published in April 1925; in May, Fitzgerald met Hemingway, and he soon began helping the younger author, recommending Ernest's work to his editor at Scribner's, Max Perkins, and to others who might help his career. This was the beginning of an odd, wary, on-again-off-again relationship that lasted until Fitzgerald's death. In many ways, the men were polar opposites, and it sometimes seemed that all they had in common was enormous talent. Hemingway had a habit of turning on his friends, and Fitzgerald could be self-pitying and, especially when drunk (which was often), either outrageous and annoying or blindly inconsiderate. Fitzgerald once said that Hemingway spoke with the authority of success, while he (Fitzgerald) spoke with the authority of failure. At least one biographer, André Le Vot, has characterized them as sadist and masochist, with all the uneasy nuances that can lend to a relationship between two highly talented, artistic men.

Hemingway's literary life was largely ahead of him at this point; his first major novel, *The Sun Also Rises,* would be published the year after *The Great Gatsby* (by Scribner's; Max Perkins had agreed with Fitzgerald's assessment of Hemingway). He would go on to win the Nobel and Pulitzer prizes. As for Fitzgerald, on the other hand, *The Great Gatsby* would represent his highest critical acclaim; nothing he published afterward would receive the same enthusiastic reception.

THE LONG SLIDE DOWNHILL

Gatsby did not sell as well as Fitzgerald would have liked, but as a stage adaptation it was a hit both on Broadway in February 1926 and later on tour. This success helped take some of the sting out of the failure of *The Vegetable,* and the income from sale of the stage rights helped Fitzgerald pay off the debts he and Zelda kept running up. For the first time he had a financial cushion, which Hemingway warned him posed a danger: Both men needed a financial incentive to force themselves to write their best work.

After *Gatsby* (and the short-story collection that followed, *All the Sad Young Men*), Fitzgerald did not publish another book for eight years. *Tender Is the Night* came out in 1934, but by then the nation was nearly half a decade into the Great Depression. It seemed that Scott had outlived his time; the new novel seemed out of step, a bit old-fashioned. Scott thought perhaps it needed a major rewriting, and he proposed massive changes. He never followed up on those ideas, but after his death, Malcolm Cowley edited a new edition, published "with the author's final revisions," so the novel now exists in two very different published forms.

Fitzgerald had tried to keep up with the times—he had even taken a couple of stabs at writing for Hollywood, with an occasional minor success—but it seemed his personal fortunes had waned with those of the previous decade. Zelda was by this time seriously ill. Her schizophrenia had finally been diagnosed, and she was spending long periods of time in mental hospitals. During intervals when she was well enough to be released, she began going home to her mother rather than to Scott; although she and Scott still wrote each other and remained affectionate, being together seemed to make them both irrational. Trying to attend to Zelda, take care of Scottie, and write dozens of short stories to pay the bills for all three of them had undoubtedly taken a toll on both Fitzgerald's time and his concentration. Worse, after about 1932, Scott found that he no longer had the facility to dash off the lucrative stories that had been supporting them for years. Whether he or the editors had changed or the times simply no longer suited his stories (he remarked that editors all wanted stories with happy endings now, and few of his stories were sufficiently upbeat anymore), he was no longer able to command top dollar, automatic publication of whatever he submitted, or even advances against future work, as he had long been accustomed to. (Nor were his books selling well: The last royalty check to arrive before he died, in August 1940, was for $13.13.)

He turned once again to Hollywood, landing a contract with MGM in mid-1937. But Fitzgerald was not a good team player when it came to literary collaboration, and he did not bother to hide his unhappiness when his work was rewritten. By the end of 1938, MGM declined to renew his contract. He was putting his time in Hollywood to use, though: He began a new novel, one he envisioned as his masterpiece, about Hollywood. Based loosely on the life of producer Irving Thalberg, he called it *The Last Tycoon.* Ill health, including cardiac problems and at least one heart attack, slowed him somewhat, but he was hoping to finish the book by mid-January 1941. On December 21, 1940, while he was relaxing and eating a chocolate bar, waiting for his physician to come by, he suddenly stood, reached for the chimney, and then slid to the floor. He had had another heart attack, and died quickly. He was buried six days later in Rockville, Maryland.

TOGETHER AGAIN

Zelda and Scott Fitzgerald had been apart for years before his death; their last time together was a disastrous trip to Cuba in 1939, where he drank heavily and was beaten by spectators at a cockfight he tried to stop. After that Zelda lived with her mother when she was well and returned to the hospital when schizophrenia threatened to overwhelm her. In March 1948 she had been hospitalized for four months and was looking forward to returning home. On the night of March 10 a fire broke out in the hospital; Zelda and eight other women were trapped and died in the flames. On March 17 she was laid to rest next to Scott.

LOOKING BACK

In 1931, at the age of thirty-five, Fitzgerald looked back wistfully at the Jazz Age, a brief period between the First World War and the Great Depression, an era of which he was both chronicler and, to many, personification. "It is too soon to write about the Jazz Age with perspective," he wrote:

> It is as dead as were the Yellow Nineties in 1902. Yet the present writer already looks back to it with nostalgia. It bore him up, flattered him and gave him more money than he had dreamed of, simply for telling people that he felt as they did, that something had to be done with all the nervous energy stored up and unexpended in the War.

CHAPTER 1

Fitzgerald as the Living Symbol of His Time

The Legend Was His Life

Alfred Kazin

In his 1942 critical work *On Native Grounds: An Interpretation of Modern Prose Literature*, author and critic Alfred Kazin explains why F. Scott Fitzgerald is so closely identified with the images of his generation, especially of the 1920s. Fitzgerald's life itself was a legend and embodied the 1920s; he was deeply absorbed in living in, and writing about, that world. Kazin also edited *F. Scott Fitzgerald: The Man and His Work*, a 1951 collection of letters and essays.

Fitzgerald, who never underwent the European apprenticeship that [his contemporaries Ernest Hemingway and John Dos Passos] did, always stood rather apart from them, though he was the historian of his generation and for a long time its most famous symbol. For Fitzgerald never had to create a lost-generation legend or apply it to literature—the exile, the pilgrimage to Gertrude Stein, the bullfighters at the extremity of the world, the carefully molded style, the carefully molded disgust. The legend actually was his life, as he was its most native voice and signal victim; and his own career was one of its great stories, perhaps its central story. From the first he lived in and for the world of his youth, the glittering and heartbroken postwar world from which his career was so indistinguishable. Living by it he became for many not so much the profoundly gifted, tragic, and erratic writer that he was, a writer in some ways inherently more interesting than any other in his generation, but a marvelous, disappointed, and disappointing child—"a kind of king of our American youth" who had long since lost his kingdom and was staggering in a void. He became too much a legend in himself, too easily a fragment of history rather than a contributor to it. And when he died in his early forties, the "snuffed-out candle," dead in that Hollywood that was his last extremity, with even one of his greatest books, *The Last Tycoon*, unfinished like his life, glittering with promise like his life, he served the legend in death as he had served it by his whole life. . . . Scott Fitzgerald was dead; the twenties were really over; the waste and folly had gone with him.

SPEAKING FOR THE MODERN GENERATION

It was almost impossible, of course, not to discount Fitzgerald in some such spirit, for he was as much a part of the twenties as Calvin Coolidge, and like Coolidge, represented something in the twenties almost too graphically. He had announced the lost generation with *This Side of Paradise* in 1920, or at least the home guard of the international rebellion of postwar youth, and the restiveness of youth at home found an apostle in him, since he was the younger generation's first authentic novelist. Flippant, ironic, chastely sentimental, he spoke for all those who felt, as one youth wrote in 1920, that "the old generation had certainly pretty well ruined this world before passing it on to us. They give us this thing, knocked to pieces, leaky, red-hot, threatening to blow up; and then they are surprised that we don't accept it with the same attitude of pretty, decorous enthusiasm with which they received it, way back in the eighties." As the flapper supplanted the suffragette, the cake-eater the earnest young uplifter of 1913, Fitzgerald came in with the modernism that flew in on short skirts, puffed audaciously at its cigarette, evinced a frantic interest in sport and sex, in drinking prohibited liquor, and in defying the ancient traditions. In 1920 he was not so much a novelist as a new generation speaking; but it did not matter. He sounded all the fashionable new lamentations; he gave the inchoate protests of his generation a slogan, a character, a definitive tone. Like Rudolph Valentino, he became one of the supreme personalities of the new day; and when his dashingly handsome hero, Amory Blaine, having survived Princeton, the war, and one tempestuous love affair, stood out at the end of the novel as a man who had conquered all the illusions and was now waiting on a lonely road to be conquered in turn, it seemed as if a generation ambitious for a sense of tragedy had really found a tragic hero.

Like Alfred de Musset's Rolla, Fitzgerald might now have said: *Je suis venu trop tard dans un monde trop vieux pour moi* [I have arrived too late into a world too old for me]—and he did, in all the variants of undergraduate solemnity and bright wisdom. With its flip and elaborately self-conscious prose, *This Side of Paradise* was a record of the younger generation's victory over *all* the illusions. The war, Amory Blaine confesses, had no great effect on him,

> but it certainly ruined the old backgrounds. Sort of killed individualism out of our whole generation. . . . I'm not sure it didn't kill it out of the whole world. Oh, Lord, what a pleasure it used to be to dream I might be a really great dictator or writer or religious or political leader—and now even a Leonardo da Vinci or Lorenzo de Medici couldn't be a real old-fashioned bolt in the world.

Knocking loudly and portentously at the locked doors of convention, Fitzgerald had already become the voice of "all the sad young men." With a sly flourish, he announced that "none of the Victorian mothers—and most of the mothers were Victorian—had any idea how casually their daughters were accustomed to be kissed." Mothers swooned and legislators orated; Fitzgerald continued to report the existence of such depravity and cynicism as they had never dreamed of. The shock was delivered; Fitzgerald became part of the postwar atmosphere of shock.

But though it was inconsequential enough, *This Side of Paradise* had a taste of the poignance that was to flood all Fitzgerald's other books. To tell all was now the fashion; flaming youth was lighting up behind every barn; but of what use was it? Behind the trivial irony of Fitzgerald's novel, its heroic pose, its grandiose dramatizations ("Amory was alone—he had escaped from a small enclosure into a great labyrinth. He was where Goethe was when he began 'Faust'; he was where Conrad was when he wrote 'Almayer's Folly'") lay a terrible fear of the contemporary world, a world young men had never made. Freedom had come, but only as a medium of expression; while some of the young men licked their war wounds, others sought certainty. "We *want* to believe, but we can't." The problem was there for all men to ponder, and for "the beautiful and the damned" to suffer. But how did one learn to believe? What was there to believe in?

A PART OF THE WORLD HIS MIND DISOWNED

Fitzgerald never found the answer, yet he did not mock those who had. In those first years he did not seek answers; perhaps he never did. As Glenway Wescott said in his tribute at the end, he "always suffered from an extreme environmental sense." He commented on the world, swam in it as self-contentedly as the new rich, and understood it sagely—when he wanted to; he had no innerness. His senses always opened outward to the world, and the world was full of Long Island Sundays. This was what he knew and was steeped in, the procession and glitter that he loved without the statement of love, and he had the touch for it—the light yet jeweled style, careless and knowing and affable; the easiness that was never facility; the holiday lights, the holiday splendor, the twenties in their golden bowl, whose crack he knew so well. He was innocent without living in innocence and delighted in the external forms and colors without being taken in by them; but he was pre-eminently a part of the world his mind was always disowning. The extravagance and carnival of the times had laid a charm on him, and he caught the carnival of the world of his youth, and its welling inaudible sadness, as no one else did—the world of Japanese lanterns and tea dances, the hot summer afternoons in *The Great Gatsby*, the dazzle and sudden violence, the colored Easter eggs whose tints got into his prose, the blare of the saxophones "while a hundred pairs of golden and silver slippers shuffled the shining dust. At the gray tea hour there were always rooms that throbbed incessantly with this low, sweet fever, while fresh faces drifted here and there like rose petals blown by the sad horns around the floor."

THE RICH: THE ARTIST'S MEDIUM OF UNDERSTANDING

Inevitably, there was a persistent tension in Fitzgerald between what his mind knew and what his spirit adhered to; between his disillusionment and his irrevocable respect for the power and the glory of the world he described. "Let me tell you about the very rich," he wrote in *All the Sad Young Men*.

> They are different from you and me. They possess and enjoy early, and it does something to them, makes them soft where we are hard, and cynical where we are trustful, in a way that, unless you were born rich, it is very difficult to understand. They think, deep in their hearts, that they are better than we are because we had to discover the compensations and refuges of life for ourselves. . . . They are different.

He was fascinated by that difference, where a writer like [American writer Joseph] Hergesheimer merely imitated it;

none of the others in his generation felt the fascination of the American success story as did Fitzgerald, or made so much of it. ("The rich are not as we are," he once said to Hemingway. "No," Hemingway replied. "They have more money.") This was the stuff of life to him, the American achievement he could recognize, and hate a little, and be forever absorbed by. And from Amory Blaine's education to Monroe Stahr's Hollywood in *The Last Tycoon*, Fitzgerald's world did radiate the Cartier jewel glints of the twenties—the diamond mountain in "The Diamond as Big as the Ritz," Anson Hunter in "The Rich Boy," Jay Gatsby's mansion and dream, the prep-school princelings who swagger through so many of his stories, the luxurious self-waste of the last expatriates in *Tender Is the Night*, and finally Monroe Stahr, the Hollywood king, "who had looked on all the kingdoms, with the kind of eye that can stare straight into the sun."

Fitzgerald did not worship riches or the rich; he merely lived in their golden eye. They were "different"; they were what the writer who lived forever in the world of his youth really knew; and they became for him what war became for Hemingway, or the anarchy of modern society for Dos Passos—the pattern of human existence, the artist's medium of understanding. His people were kings; they were imperious even in their desolation. They were always the last of their line, always damned, always the death-seekers (there are no second generations in Fitzgerald). Yet they were glamorous to the end, as the futilitarians in *Tender Is the Night* and Monroe Stahr were iridescent with death. For Fitzgerald always saw life as glamour, even though he could pierce that glamour to write one of the most moving of American tragedies in *The Great Gatsby*. Something of a child always, with a child's sudden and unexpected wisdom, he could play with the subtle agonies of the leisure class as with a brilliant toy; and the glamour always remained there, even when it was touched with death. In one sense, as a magazine writer once put it, his books were "prose movies," and nothing was more characteristic of his mind than his final obsession with Hollywood. In the same way much of his writing always hovered on the verge of fantasy and shimmered with all the colors of the world. Just as the world swam through his senses without being defined by him, so he could catch all its lights and tones in his prismatic style without having to understand them too consciously. What saved his style from extravagance was Fitzgerald's special grace, his pride in his craft; but it was the style of a man profoundly absorbed in the romance of glamour, the style of a craftsman for whom life was a fairy world to the end.

FITZGERALD BELONGED TO GATSBY'S WORLD

To understand this absorption on Fitzgerald's part is to understand the achievement of *The Great Gatsby*, the work by which his name will always live. In most of his other work he merely gave shallow reports on the pleasures and self-doubts of his class, glittered with its glitter. He tended to think of his art as a well-oiled machine, and he trusted to luck. Rather like Stephen Crane, whom he so much resembled in spirit, the only thing he could be sure of was his special gift, his way of transfusing everything with words, the consciousness of craft; and like Crane he made it serve for knowledge. But like Crane in another respect, he was one of those writers who make their work out of a conflict that would paralyze others—out of their tragic moodiness, their troubled, intuitive, and curiously half-conscious penetration of the things before them. And it is this moodiness at the pitch of genius that lights up *The Great Gatsby*. For Fitzgerald was supremely a part of the world he there described, weary of it but not removed from it, and his achievement was of a kind possible only to one who so belonged to it. No revolutionary writer could have written it, or even hinted at its inexpressible poignance; no one, perhaps, who was even too consciously skeptical of the wealth and power Jay Gatsby thought would make him happy. But for Fitzgerald the tragedy unfolded there, the tragedy that has become for so many one of the great revelations of what it has meant to be an American at all, was possible only because it was so profound a burst of self-understanding.

To have approached Gatsby from the outside would have meant a sacrifice of Gatsby himself—a knowledge of everything in Gatsby's world save Gatsby. But the tragedy here is pure confession, a supplication complete in the human note it strikes. Fitzgerald could sound the depths of Gatsby's life because he himself could not conceive any other. Out of his own weariness and fascination with damnation he caught Gatsby's damnation, caught it as only someone so profoundly attentive to Gatsby's dream could have pierced to the self-lie behind it. The book has no real scale; it does not rest on any commanding vision, nor is it in any sense a major tragedy. But it is a great flooding moment, a moment's intimation and penetration; and as Gatsby's disillusion becomes felt at the end it strikes like a chime through the mind. It was as if Fitzgerald, the playboy moving with increasing despair through this tinsel world of Gatsby's, had reached that perfect moment, before the break of darkness and death, when the mind does really and absolutely know itself—a moment when only those who have lived by Gatsby's great illusion, lived by the tinsel and the glamour, can feel the terrible force of self-betrayal. This was the playboy's rare apotheosis, and one all the more moving precisely because all of Gatsby's life was summed up in it, precisely because his decline and death gave a meaning to his life that it had not in itself possessed.

Here was the chagrin, the waste of the American success story in the twenties: here, in a story that was a moment's revelation. Yet think, Fitzgerald seems to say to us, of how little Gatsby wanted at bottom—not to understand society, but to ape it; not to compel the world, but to live in it. His own dream of wealth meant nothing in itself; he merely wanted to buy back the happiness he had lost—Daisy, now the rich man's wife—when he had gone away to war. So the great Gatsby house at West Egg glittered with all the lights of the twenties, and there were always parties, and always Gatsby's supplicating hand, reaching out to make out of glamour what he had lost by the cruelty of chance. "Gatsby believed in the green light, the orgiastic future that year by year recedes before us. It eluded us then, but that's no matter—tomorrow we will run faster, stretch out our arms farther. . . . And one fine morning—" So the great Gatsby house, Gatsby having failed in his dream, now went out with all its lights, save for that last unexpected and uninvited guest whom Nick heard at the closed Gatsby door one night, the guest "who had been away at the ends of the earth and didn't know that the party was over." And now there was only the wry memory of Gatsby's dream, left in that boyhood schedule of September 12, 1906, with its promise of industry and self-development—"Rise from bed. . . . Study electricity . . . work. . . . Practice elocution and how to attain it. . . . Read one improving book or magazine per week." So all the lights of Fitzgerald's golden time went out with Jay Gatsby—Gatsby, the flower of the republic, the bootlegger who made the American dream his own, and died by it. "So we beat on, boats against the current, borne back ceaselessly into the past."

THE MOST GIFTED AND SELF-DESTRUCTIVE OF THE LOST BOYS

Gatsby's was Fitzgerald's apotheosis, too. As the haunting promise of *The Last Tycoon* testifies, he did not lose his skill; there is a grim poetic power in his unraveling of Monroe Stahr greater in itself than anything else in his work. But something in Fitzgerald died concurrently with the dying of his world. His fairy world decomposed slowly, lingeringly; and he lived with its glitter, paler and paler, to the end. Writing what he himself called "the novel of deterioration" in *Tender Is the Night*, he kept to the glow, the almost hereditary grace, that was so natural for him. But he lavished it upon a world of pure emptiness there; he was working away in the pure mathematics of sensation. The subtlety of his last books was a fever glow, a neurotic subtlety. He had always to return to the ancient dream of youth and power, the kings who always died in his work but were kings nevertheless—the dominating men, the ornate men, the imperials in whose light he lived because they were the romantic magnifications of the world of his youth. And reading that painful confession of his own collapse, the essay smuggled away in *Esquire* which he called "The Crack-Up," one felt how fantastic it was, as Glenway Westcott put it in his tender tribute to Fitzgerald, "that a man who is dying or at least done with living—one who has had practically all that the world affords, fame and prosperity, work and play, love and friendship, and lost practically all—should still think seriously of so much fiddledeedee of boyhood." But Fitzgerald was a boy, the most startlingly gifted and self-destructive of all the lost boys, to the end. There is an intense brooding wisdom, all Fitzgerald's keen sense of craft raised and burnished to new power, in *The Last Tycoon* that is unforgettable. To see how he could manipulate the emergence of Stahr's power and sadness, the scene of the airplane flight from New York to Hollywood and the moment when the earthquake trembled in Hollywood, is to appreciate how much closer Fitzgerald could come than most modern American novelists to fulfillment, of a kind. But what is Monroe Stahr—the Hollywood producer "who had looked on all the kingdoms," who died so slowly and glitteringly all through the book as Fitzgerald did in life—but the last, the most feverishly concentrated of Fitzgerald's fairy-world characters in that Hollywood that was the final expression of the only world Fitzgerald ever knew? Fitzgerald could penetrate Hollywood superbly; he could turn his gift with the easiest possible dexterity on anything he touched. But he did not touch very much. With all his skill (it is odd to think that where he was once too easily passed off as the desperate Punch of his generation, he may now be rated as a master craftsman in a day worshipful of craftsmanship), Fitzgerald's world is a little one, a superior boy's world—precocious in its wisdom, precocious in its tragedy, but the fitful glaring world of Jay Gatsby's dream, and of Jay Gatsby's failure, to the end.

Historian of
Interlocking Worlds

Malcolm Bradbury

Novelist and critic Malcolm Bradbury sees F. Scott
Fitzerald as playing a dual role. Fitzgerald was both
a participant and chronicler, Bradbury notes, able to
immerse himself in the world as well as write objec-
tively about it. From *This Side of Paradise* to *The Last
Tycoon* (left unfinished at Fitzgerald's death), Bradbury traces a maturing author as he reflects, and
later reflects on, the various and contrasting aspects
of his world.

No writer set out more determinedly to capture in fiction the
tone, the hope, the possibility, and the touch of despair of the
Twenties than Francis Scott Key Fitzgerald. For a long time
he appeared to his critics a mere popularizer and chronicler,
so obviously immersed in the themes, fashions, and styles of
his times that he never achieved the literary power to consider and criticize. Certainly the writer who made a fortune
for performing the Twenties in public, who was so readily
allured by the wonder of the rich and the dream of success,
was more than most novelists an author who lived and
worked through immersion in his own public world. For this
he finally paid a high cost, to his famous marriage to Zelda
Sayre, to his psychic life, to his writing and his reputation. It
often seemed that the glittering style of his books, encrusted
with beautiful women and wealthy heroes, was no more
than a version of the glittering popular name he sought for
himself, that his preoccupation with the all-inclusive hero,
the man who embodies all the hopes and dreams of those
around him, was an expression of the self he sought to be.
And Fitzgerald undoubtedly threw himself exotically into
the pleasures and the pitfalls of his own gaudy time; he was,
more than most, an essentially social novelist. It was he who

made sure that the Twenties was known as 'the Jazz Age', that the new goods and chattels, the new expressions and sexual styles, made their way into fiction. His famous essay 'The Crack-Up' sums up this singular identification. The historical development of America in the 1920s, moving from glittering excitement to danger, was his own psychic curve; the Great Crash [stock market crash of 1929] was the exact analogue of his own psychic crack up; the political reassessment of the Thirties was the match for his own endeavour to put his spiritual house in order. Such identifications were so potent exactly because Fitzgerald always chose to live them as such, making his literary experimentation part of the period's social and sexual experimentation, making the style of his life an essential component of the style of his art. This made his work itself appear innocent, his writing seem short of formal skill. It has taken time for us to see that there was much more, and that the innocent performer of the Twenties became, in his mature work, one of the finest of modern American novelists.

CHILD OF THE NEW CENTURY

Fitzgerald was born in Saint Paul, Minnesota, in September, 1896, and saw himself as a child of the new century. A Midwesterner of Maryland stock, he went back East as soon as he could in quest of the life of the East Coast patriciate from which he felt himself to be descended. It takes a true provincial to see the charm and glow of status and wealth, and Fitzgerald, the aspiring young man from Summit Avenue, St Paul, was always drawn by the golden glow in the East. When he went to Princeton in 1913 he entered a world that was all promise, wealth, and dream; that parvenu[1] dream would be the most fabulous of the stories he had to tell. The other key story was the story of a generation. When, in 1917, he was working on the novel he then called *The Romantic Egoist* and would be published as *This Side of Paradise*, he wrote grandly to his friend Edmund Wilson, 'I really believe that no one else could have written so searchingly the story of the youth of our generation . . .'. *This Side of Paradise* came out in 1920, exactly as the Twenties started, and became an immediate bestseller, rivalling in the lists a work by another Minnesotan, Sinclair Lewis's *Main Street*. But where Lewis

1. newly arrived and unaccustomed to wealth

satirized the American vanities of the Twenties, Fitzgerald offered an entirely different, quite unsatirical view of the world of post-war modernity. Heavily influenced by Compton Mackenzie's now little-read *Sinister Street*, it followed the period vogue for young men's novels; its young hero, Amory Blaine, is the exemplary post-war dandy, socially and sexually ambitious, who makes his own life the subject of a social and aesthetic experiment, conducted through the pursuit of religion, love, and money. Amory is indeed a 'romantic egoist', drawn on the one hand by a narcissistic investment in his own youth and beauty, and on the other by all the dreamy and fragile promises society and immersion in experience can offer him. Above all there is Princeton's 'glittering caste-system' and the beautiful and wealthy woman who embodies all he desires but stands just beyond his reach. Style becomes a desperate expenditure of the self, and beauty and money turn into transposed versions of each other. Far more energetic than good, the book none the less lays down, if in unresolved form, many of the themes that would subsequently dominate his fiction: the temptation, danger, and damnation of self-love, an awareness of the alluring fragility of all experience, and a compulsive neo-religious idealism that, invested back into American society, somehow attempts to make it shine with a transcendental glory—the themes he would eventually bring into perfect focus in *The Great Gatsby*.

With characteristic honesty Fitzgerald was later to identify the book as 'one of the funniest books since *Dorian Gray* in its utter speciousness', but it was a work that signalled to a generation its presence as a generation, and its remarkable unexpected success threw Fitzgerald into a role he coveted—the style-setter for the times, the filter and promoter of its public moods and sexual fashions. It also enabled him to marry his remote woman, Zelda Sayre, and together the two of them went on to perform the Twenties as an exotic dance of romance and decadent cynicism, as they chased the excitements, spent the wealth, drank the champagne, travelled, enjoyed the playboy delights, and equally consumed the underlying moral and economic fragility. Zelda (eventually a novelist herself) was the new woman, the flapper displaying the boyish toughness, sexual ambiguity, and moral vagueness of a time of changing sexual roles. Scott was equally the new man, capturing style in all its topicality and writing for 'my own personal public—that is, the countless flappers and college kids who think I am a sort of oracle'. Their expensive transatlantic life forced Fitzgerald to write against the clock, in several senses, and he found problems in distancing himself from his own stories or finding time to develop his talent. The titles of his next books of stories—*Flappers and Philosophers* (1920), *Tales from the Jazz Age* (1922)—show his obsession with capturing the period themes. At the same time he was capable of giving his stories a serious treatment and, as he noted, the stories all 'had a touch of disaster in them; the lovely young creatures in my novels went to ruin, the diamond mountains of my short stories blew up, my millionaires were as beautiful and damned as Thomas Hardy's peasants.' That touch of disaster is very clear in his next novel, *The Beautiful and Damned* (1922), a story about a degenerating hero and a degenerating marriage, which mixes social lyricism with a tale of decadent decline. Gloria and Anthony Patch want to make their marriage into a 'live, lovely, glamorous performance', based on the American premise that 'something is going to happen'. But false dreams, moral carelessness, and the pressure of time soon take their toll: 'I don't want to live without my pretty face,' cries Gloria. Hastily written and heavily autobiographical, the book—though perfectly successful—lacks a confident tone, and there was little about it to suggest that his next work would be one of the greatest American novels, the book T.S. Eliot would identify as 'the first step the American novel has taken since Henry James.'

A WRITER IMMERSED IN HIS TIMES

But by now Fitzgerald was growing increasingly conscious of having squandered his talents, and as he began his next book he determined to show himself the conscious artist he believed he could be. That book consequently displays a new seriousness, sometimes explained by the critics as showing for the first time he could stand back and survey his own experience. Yet if anything Fitzgerald's sense of his immersion in his times had increased; just like his character Dick Diver in *Tender Is the Night* (1934), who feels compelled to risk his own sanity and intelligence in order to understand and redeem the crisis consciousness of others, he saw it as the writer's task to be a 'performing self', as it has been called, an active agent taking risks with his life and entering all the places where the times are most fully enacted. Both his personal and fictional styles were modes of involvement; but now, in his better work, he began increasingly to understand the compelling forces behind this psychic overextension. With *The Great Gatsby* (1925), one of the most notable of American twentieth-century novels, this mixture of involvement and understanding reaches an extraordinary balance. The book is a classic of formal control (Fitzgerald had learned it in part from Joseph Conrad); it is also a book that seeks exactly to enter its own time and place while reaching beyond it—just as its central character, Jay Gatsby, aims to do. It is the story of a gross, materialistic, careless society of coarse wealth spread on top of a sterile world; on to it is cast an extraordinary illusion, that of the ex-Jay Gatz, the self-created Gatsby. A man whose poor past and corrupt economic supports are hidden in his own glow, Gatsby likewise decorates his entire world through his love for Daisy Buchanan. Society is decadent in one way, Gatsby in another: he is a dandy of desire, a desire that has been redirected from its human or material object into a fantasy, a dream of retaining a past moment in an endless instant of contemplation. His aim, in effect, is to transfigure money into love—a symbolist dream, an assault on reality, the system, the clock of time itself. The clock still ticks, and Fitzgerald hears it; Gatsby is a corrupt dreamer, Daisy a corrupt object of love, married to a violent, damaging husband, surrounded by 'carelessness' and social indifference, her voice full of money. But he grants the grandeur of the invented self and the gaudy worth of its passions: 'The most grotesque and fantastic conceits haunted [Gatsby] in his bed at night. A universe of ineffable gaudiness spun itself out in his brain while the clock ticked on the wash-stand and the moon soaked with wet light his tangled clothes upon the floor.' Gatsby embodies the symbolic aim of the book itself, a figure floating on the American dream while beneath him a confusing record of economic and social facts unravels.

Gatsby is a coarse Platonist, devoted to the pursuit of a 'vast, vulgar and meretricious beauty', but his dream sustains its force, partly because the book allows him to invest naturalist fact with his personal intention, and recognizes symbolist desires, and partly because it is mediated through a narrator, Nick Carraway, who consciously stills the voice of judgement. Carraway's peculiar tolerance comes because he is himself involved in a fantastic life in which he is something of a parvenu, but also because he is the instrument of Fitzgerald's oblique method of interpreting the tale. *Gatsby* is a novel of modern dream-life; and its means call for something more than naturalism or direct moral assessment. It is itself a semi-symbolist text, set in the surreal world of the modern city, New York and its environs, its startling detail thrown up in instants and images in the shifting fashions in clothes and music, the décor of hotel rooms, the movements of traffic, the ash heaps and the hearses that catch Carraway's eye on his mobile, hyperactive way through the populous landscape. As narrator, Carraway becomes a voice of what Fitzgerald called 'selective delicacy', filtering impression and sensation in an order appropriate to his growing understanding of Gatsby's nature, distributing about him a landscape of generative images, so that Gatsby, who might be thought of as a corrupt product of this world, is gradually distinguished from it, set against it, finally made a victim of its carelessness. The novel's theme is the suffusion of the material with the ideal, of raw stuff becoming enchanted object. This is so not just because of Gatsby's peculiar powers and qualities, but because it is the basis of the mode of writing itself, as it invests Gatsby's actions, parties, and clothes with a distinctive, symbolic glow.

ALTERNATIVE, CONTRASTING WORLDS

Two alternative worlds, one of careless wealth and the other of ashen poverty, are set in contrast in the novel—watched over by the absent god, the sightless eyes of Dr Eckleberg. But the real contrast is between the contingency of both these worlds and Gatsby's search for a transfiguring vision, for a world beyond the clock of historical time, for a life meaningless unless invested with meaning. Fitzgerald's aim is surreal, the making bright of certain evanescent things so that they have the quality of dream. But at the novel's end that dream is withdrawn, and another surreality, the nightmare of an unmitigated mass of material objects, takes its place. Gatsby's death is the product of carelessness and chance. Nick imagines it:

> I have an idea that Gatsby didn't himself believe that it [the phone call from Daisy] would come, and perhaps he no longer cared. If that was true he must have felt that he had lost the old warm world, paid a high a price for living so long

with a single dream. He must have looked up at an unfamiliar sky through frightening leaves and shivered as he found
what a grotesque thing a rose is and how raw the sunlight
was upon scarcely created grass. A new world, material without being real, where poor ghosts, breathing dreams like air,
drifted fortuitously about . . . like the ashen, fantastic figure
gliding toward him through the amorphous trees.

On the one hand there is the world of time arrested, the past
held suspended, of love and dream: on the other there is a
modern world of dislocated, rootless, and grotesque images.
From the mixture Fitzgerald distills two essential compo-
nents of modernist writing. The book made him the extraordinary historian of those two interlocking worlds—the world
of modern history invested with a timeless myth, where the
clock is tilted back like the clock on Gatsby's mantelpiece as
he kisses Daisy, and the world of history disinvested, reduced to fragments without manifest order, a modern waste
land. This tension and ambiguity persist into the famous
ending, where Fitzgerald both recreates 'the American
dream', the dream of an innocent, pastoral America created
by man's capacity for wonder, and also sees it as a nostalgic
desire for that which time itself defeats. As Gatsby is an artistic surrogate, chasing with his 'creative passion' a symbol
that is both transcendent and corrupted, *The Great Gatsby* is
a symbolist tragedy—about the struggle of the symbolic
imagination to exist in lowered historical time, and about
that symbol's inherent ambiguity, its wonder and its mere-
triciousness.

Gatsby is probably Fitzgerald's best, certainly his most
finished, book: a realization of his talents in the Twenties, a
sign of his power to enter a world both gaudy and destructive and distill a meaning from it. He had succeeded not just
in internalizing the times—the spirit of a 'whole race going
hedonistic, deciding on pleasure'—but in realizing them as
form. But, as Twenties unease grew, Fitzgerald internalized
that too, sensing the economic cost to be charged, the moral
interest due. Though it was a formal success, *Gatsby* was not
a financial one. Fitzgerald now had to undertake the production of countless popular magazine short stories to
maintain his life-style, delaying his next novel, which was in
any case going through many drafts. Behind the public
façade, the marriage to Zelda was now strained, as each
fought for self-preservation and survival. The Crash of 1929

destroyed the symbolic base of their existence, and by 1930 what was latent in the inner politics of that marriage— Zelda's schizophrenia, Scott's alcoholism—was evident. 'No ground under our feet', he noted in his ledger, as the life-style they had both promoted began to tear to pieces. He now began to read Spengler, Henry Adams, Freud, and Marx, and sensed the need for a 'Great Change'. He grew aware of the historical displacement of the rich, looked towards the roots of his own wealth, began to grant the reality of the historical process and to probe the sexual disorder of the times.

A NOVEL OF PSYCHIC DISORIENTATION

All this went into the plan for his next novel, *Tender Is the Night*, a troubled and troublesome book of which we have two versions. Fitzgerald described it as follows: 'Show a man who is a natural idealist, a spoiled priest, giving in for various causes to the ideas of the haute Burgeoise [*sic*], and in his rise to the top of the social world losing his idealism, his talent and turning to drink and dissipation. Background is one in which the liesure [*sic*] class is at their truly most brilliant & glamorous.'[2] The background is the expatriate, socialite French Riviera where Americans gather, art and wealth converge, the great gaudy spree goes on past its season, and a post-war generation attempts to reconstruct an existence after the war has shelled the old society to death. But cause is divorced from effect, and on the map of modern disturbed geography amusement lies next to *Angst*, the French Riviera close to the Swiss psychiatric clinics in which the price is paid. *Tender Is the Night* is a novel of psychic disorientation, seen not only as itself, but in relation to the processes of history—thus, says Fitzgerald, 'At that moment, the Divers [his central couple] represented externally the exact furthermost evolution of a class.' The book is set in a world of chance, violence, and unexplained deaths, with echoes of the war sounding constantly in the background. The method is panoramic and expository, but historical scope is related to an inner violence and despair—above all to the insanity of Nicole Diver and the way this implicates

2. Fitzgerald's 'General Plan' for the book, reprinted as Appendix B in Arthur Mizener, *The Far Side of Paradise* (1951; rev. edn., 1965). A revised edition of *Tender Is the Night*, edited by Malcolm Cowley and incorporating some of Fitzgerald's own ideas for the book's rearrangement, appeared in 1951. The complicated history of the text is analysed in Matthew J. Bruccoli, *The Compostion of 'Tender Is the Night'* (1963).

her husband, the psychiatrist Dick Diver, the modern sav-
iour who seeks to heal the pains and bear the burdens of
these rich disintegrating psyches in a disintegrating, sexually confused, and perverse world. Like Gatsby, Dick attempts to unify the chaos and give a meaning to the disorder.
Like Gatsby, he is an idealized hero, a man with a 'fine glowing surface' who distills bright moments of transcendence,
making life into a successful and ever-moving party. Diver is
the master stylist—'there was a pleasingness about him that
simply had to be used'—and much of the early part of the
novel is about his powers of unification, his capacity to make
the world fall into place for others. His powers are more than
psychiatric, they are sacral. He blesses the world he enters,
and is indeed its 'spoiled priest'.

But to do this Diver must indeed dive into this collapsing
historical world, must risk his initial integrity—'He knew . . .
that the price of his intactness was incompleteness'—and his
illusions—'they were the illusions of a nation, the lies of generations of frontier mothers who had to croon falsely that
there were no wolves outside the cabin door'—in the chaotic,
war-shattered life of his times. Marrying Nicole, one of his
patients, wealthy and corrupt, he assimilates her mixture of
amusement and pain. His humanism becomes tarnished, his
disintegration slowly begins. A redemptive figure at the start,
at the end he is broken by drink, violence, and emotional
strain. No longer able to perform the symbolic trick—once
done with elegant ease—of lifting a man on his back while
surfing, he fades from the significant history of the book in its
last pages. Like Fitzgerald, he becomes the implicated man,
and the implication draws him into the heart of the disaster,
the psychic overextension, that is now Fitzgerald's essential
theme. The book's awareness is psychological, social, and
economic all at once; what we see is a top surface, a world of
individuals propelled by underlying processes into expres-
sive action which reveals what those processes imply. *Tender
Is the Night* differs from *Gatsby* in having two methods of pre-
sentation. One is spatial-symbolic, a method appropriate to
the priestly artist-figure at the book's centre who is seeking to
hold on to romantic integrity and wholeness amid destructive time. The other is historical-evolutionary, the story of
that time as system, a developing history with which Fitzgerald was not attentively concerned. Process and symbol struggle to give the novel an oblique chronology, and Fitzgerald

was never sure of its true order of construction. In fact he began to amend it even after publication, which is why the contemporary reader now has the original and a reconstructed text to choose between.

THE GREAT AMERICAN DREAM-FACTORY

The novel's incompleteness has a certain appropriateness; for incompleteness and exposure were now a main concern. In the notable essays of 1936 and 1937, 'The Crack-Up' and 'Early Success', he looked at the disintegration of his earlier style in life and art, playing his thirties against his twenties, the Thirties against the Twenties, distilling his concern with exterior and inward dissolution. By now the alcoholism was serious, Zelda was in a mental hospital, and Fitzgerald turned towards Hollywood for a job as screenwriter. His last novel—*The Last Tycoon* (1941)—set there, is yet more incomplete; the book was left unfinished at his early death in 1940. But evidently it was to tell a story similar to that of *Tender Is the Night*, the story of another master stylist and integrative man, destroyed by disintegrative forces in the external world and in his own emotional life. But where *Tender Is the Night* had been expository and extended, *The Last Tycoon* would reach back towards some of the methods of *Gatsby*: surrealistic concentration on scene, and use of the first-person narrator, so that the action is seen through Cecilia Brady, the rich Bennington College junior with an ironic view of Hollywood but in love with Monroe Stahr, the 'last tycoon'. Again there would be a bonding of image and age, consciousness and economics. Hollywood, the setting, is the great dream-factory of American illusions—Nathanael West was also displaying its surrealist significance in *The Day of the Locust* (1939). Stahr, the last of the great producers, living among these distorted and manufactured images, attempting to retain command, is a man who 'had just managed to climb out of a thousand years of Jewry into the late eighteenth century', and who cherishes 'the parvenu's passionate loyalty to an imaginary past'. He is at the end of his period of possible existence: unionization, modern complexity, contemporary disintegration threaten him, and he is the now-failing hero: 'There was no world so but had its heroes, and Stahr was the hero. . . . The old loyalties were trembling now, and there were clay feet everywhere; but still he was their man, the last of the princes.'

Like *The Day of the Locust, The Last Tycoon* is a classic novel of cultural images caught at a point of extreme distortion. History too has become distorted in the modern dream-factory world. Stahr is compared to past American Presidents, the princes who must relate their inner lives to public needs and fantasies. But Andrew Jackson's home is closed, and a man dies on its steps, while Abraham Lincoln appears in the commissary, 'his kindly face fixed on a forty-cent dinner, including dessert, his shawl wrapped around him as if to protect himself from the erratic air-cooling.' An absurdist, half-finished landscape of plasticized dreams and desires surrounds Stahr, and is part of him, outward history and inward psychic world. Apocalyptic disturbances overtake him; at the beginning of the book is a grotesque scene where an earthquake sends a flood sweeping through the studio lot, carrying a floating head of Siva on which two 'survivors' ride. From the head descends a woman who bears the face of Stahr's dead wife—a woman he now pursues through a sequence of transitory, fragmented scenes, as one might decadently pursue both survival and death itself. The book is made of such concentrated images, and predicts Stahr's downfall—tragedy set in waning history. The tragedy was in a sense Fitzgerald's own. A writer who had always struggled with the problem of unifying form and time, art and process, hoping to find a romantic and a moral value, he had watched the old dream of wealth and wonder redeemed pushed to extremity. Moreover his career was declining, his sensitivities were raw, and he had intimations of his own coming death. *The Last Tycoon* as we have it, unfinished, ends with a work note he had written to himself: 'ACTION IS CHARACTER'—a fair epitaph for a writer who had struggled through living to generate an experimental form for modern experience.

Rewriting the Capitalist Fable

Jonas Spatz

Fitzgerald's major theme—especially in *The Great Gatsby* and *The Last Tycoon*—is the relationship between past and present, writes author and English professor Jonas Spatz. The past is the American dream, an ideal of individualism and unlimited economic freedom, Spatz suggests; the present is the death of that dream. In *Gatsby* Fizgerald parodies the Horatio Alger/American dream theme of great success through hard work, but the successful "capitalists" are crooks. In *Tycoon* he analyzes the inability of individuals to achieve wealth and power without becoming greedy and tyrannical.

It is evident, as many have noted, that F. Scott Fitzgerald's best work is deeply indebted to the tradition of success literature in America and that in Hollywood he discovered a perfect vehicle for the expression of his own version of the capitalist myth. Particularly in *The Great Gatsby* and *The Last Tycoon*, Fitzgerald recognized that the figure of the solitary capitalist was crucial in the statement of his major theme: the relationship between past and present. The past of the three major novels is the world of the American dream—of frontier individualism, economic independence, and inspired democratic leadership. It is a younger and more romantic world, somehow simpler, more honest, and yet with "a grandeur unmatched in the present." Thus the sense of loss that unites all of Fitzgerald's fiction is not only individual; it is national and even universal. The New World, once the last outpost of hope, has been corrupted by the materialism of the industrial age.

But less apparent is the fact that as Fitzgerald matured, his attitude toward Hollywood and its relation to the Ameri-

From Jonas Spatz, "Fitzgerald, Hollywood, and the Myth of Success," in *The Thirties: Fiction, Poetry, Drama*, edited by Warren French (DeLand, FL: Everett/Edwards, 1976). Reprinted by permission of the author.

can experience became increasingly complex. At first he saw in Hollywood the contemporary image of the New World, a vulgar reflection of the reduced stature of modern man. Finally he romanticized Hollywood's history, emphasizing in the contrast between the old and new tycoons the gap between the old vision of the American dream and its present reality.

Similarly, Fitzgerald became more sympathetic toward the myth of success. At first he satirized America's economic history and lampooned its financial leaders. Later he romanticized the "grandeur" of the dream and its followers and shifted his attack to their descendants whose greed had all but buried the heroic vision. Thus each of his heroes is doomed to failure in a brutal world no longer "commensurate to his capacity for wonder." The central tragedy is not merely the death of a superior individual whose idealism is unsuited to his time but, more significantly, the loss of all idealism.

VARIATIONS ON A THEME

Fitzgerald's interest in Hollywood and the myth of success found its earliest expression in "The Diamond as Big as the Ritz." John T. Unger, a student in a fashionable prep school, is invited to a classmate's home "in the West." There he discovers that his friend's father, Braddock Washington, is the richest man in the world and that he owns a mountain which is really a diamond as large as the Ritz-Carlton Hotel. The rest of the story describes the infinite splendor of the estate, which could have been designed only by a Hollywood producer—the only man "used to playing with an unlimited amount of money, though he did tuck his napkin in his collar and couldn't read or write." The estate has been built entirely upon the selfishness and brutality of the pioneer Washingtons who found the mountain, exploited it, and killed trespassers to hide its existence. Braddock Washington is the epitome of the American tycoon and a prototype for many later Hollywood caricatures. He maintains his empire through slavery and violence, and in the ironic climax of the story, in order to protect his land from invasion, he attempts to bribe God to turn back the clock. Washington's madness, however, is only a logical extension of the Gospel of Wealth. The history of his family is the history of the American dream in the nineteenth century, and his complete disregard for human values is merely modern capitalism in action. The story is also a condemnation of the hollow luxury that money can buy, a reduction to absurdity of the dream of wealth and power. Washington's estate is like a colossal movie set, the ultimate in bourgeois vulgarity and an image of the American dream itself. At the end of the tale, the hero survives and learns that maturity means a disenchantment with material values. In this early story, Fitzgerald relates Hollywood to the tasteless luxury and the despotic power of the myth of success.

Fitzgerald's later work is a variation on this basic pattern. Both *The Great Gatsby* and *The Last Tycoon* contain a kind of romantic triangle between the hero, his antagonist, and the image of the American dream. James Gatz and Monroe Stahr are two self-made men, the last of a breed of believers in individualism and unlimited economic freedom. Set against them are the cruel and hostile figures of Tom Buchanan and Pat Brady—symbols of the materialism and selfishness that have perverted these ideals. In each case, the prize is a combination of youth, romance, beauty, and wealth constituting the dream. In *Gatsby* this complex is embodied in the person of Daisy, without whom Gatsby's life was "material without being real." In *The Last Tycoon* the symbol is Hollywood, Stahr's empire, the vehicle of his intense hope.

THE CAPITALIST MYTH

Not until we have read through almost all of *The Great Gatsby* does it become apparent that the novel is a continuation of Fitzgerald's treatment of the capitalist myth. Gatsby's career is a parody of the Horatio Alger theme. His boyhood schedule, prescribing the balanced and sober life that Benjamin Franklin had cited as "the way to wealth," illustrates his early commitment to the dream of success. With unintentional insight, his father compares him to the notorious robber baron, James J. Hill ("He'd of helped build up the country.") Dedicated to his destiny, like some god, he "sprang from his Platonic conception of himself." And like an Alger hero, he strikes his luck first through the whim of a benefactor, the last of the "pioneer debauchers," and later, in a grotesque shift of fortune, in association with "the man who fixed the World Series." Sometime between that boyhood resolution and his rise to fortune the dream of wealth and beauty had been corrupted. Gatsby tells Nick a "Hollywood" tale of his past, vainly pretending that he has actually fulfilled his early expectations. Like the robber barons, he has become a parvenu, living in isolation, throwing wild and vulgar parties in an attempt to recapture his youthful idealism—that is, to meet Daisy again. In making her admit to Tom that she never loved him, Gatsby attempts to repeat the past, to recapture Daisy as she was, and to recover "some idea of himself perhaps that had gone into loving Daisy." But he fails to realize that his dream is "already behind him, somewhere back in that vast obscurity beyond the city," in the vanished paradise of the New World.

But there is a greater tragedy in the novel than either Gatsby's blindness or his lost virtue. Just as Gatsby's earlier associations represent the destruction of his innocence, Daisy becomes the symbol of the central irony of the novel: the expectation and disillusionment of the dream of success. Once she had embodied beauty and romance and his youthful desire. He returns to find only that "her voice is full of money." He discovers in her a shallow greed, reflecting his own failure to live up to his ideals. Although he desires her "beyond wealth," she chooses Tom Buchanan, "a hulking brute," a bigot, a defender of "art" and "civilization" against the colored peril. Tom's doctrine of racial superiority and his social irresponsibility suggest the Social Darwinism which, Fitzgerald believed, had already undermined the innocence of capitalism. Tom converts Daisy to his values, and her denial of Gatsby is America's refusal to honor its past. The prize is no longer worthy of the heroism of its empire builders. The new tycoons will reap the spoils of a stolen world.

This comparison of past and present is reinforced in sexual terms. Daisy was "the first nice girl" that Gatsby had met, but on his return he realizes that his battle with Tom is on sexual grounds, a test of masculinity that Gatsby must ultimately fail. Tom is unfaithful to Daisy, but their physical relationship has long ago erased the memory of her former experience with Gatsby. The loss of moral innocence in the novel is parallel to the loss of sexual innocence and the rejection of the conventions of romantic love.

Nick finally concludes that the novel's characters, all Midwesterners, had some deficiency which made them "subtly unadaptable to Eastern life." That is, as survivors of an agrarian past, they are unable to cope with urban society that is grinding American ideals under the heel of materialism. Thus on one level, the novel can be read as a capitalist fable with an unhappy ending. Yet Fitzgerald departs from the attitude of "The Diamond as Big as the Ritz," since he is essentially sympathetic to Gatsby, who, after all, belongs to the same race as Braddock Washington. Like Gatsby, capitalism has been a victim of its own success. For the first time Fitzgerald shares in its expectation and weeps at its defeat.

THE MYTH OF HOLLYWOOD JOINS THE MYTH OF SUCCESS

Seen in this somewhat restricted light, *The Great Gatsby* is a logical predecessor to *The Last Tycoon*. Apparently Fitzgerald intended to portray in more detail a hero of the same type as Gatsby. *The Last Tycoon* is more specific about the forces in modern America which threaten to destroy men like Gatsby and Monroe Stahr. It is a less symbolic, less suggestive novel, but it successfully combines the myth of success with the myth of Hollywood. Fitzgerald adapted the capitalist theme to a real economic situation and transferred to Hollywood all the symbolic overtones in Daisy's character.

In *The Last Tycoon*, Fitzgerald attempts to analyze the capitalist myth in terms of those who most believed in it and built an industry on it. Monroe Stahr represents the old Hollywood and the frontier phase in American history. He is the most complete of Fitzgerald's Horatio Alger heroes, yet unlike the classic nineteenth century tycoon, and like most Hollywood leaders, he is a Jew. We learn almost nothing about Stahr's youth, but the central features of the myth are present. Brought up on the streets of the Bronx with little education, he was a born leader, a "frail boy" walking "always at the head of the gang . . . occasionally throwing a command backward out of the corner of his mouth." Like Theodore Dreiser's Cowperwood he had wanted to be the chief clerk, "to know where everything was," but his ambition has made him much more than that. Fitzgerald, in his notes, describes Stahr as a "scrapper, one of the boys, a boy destined to succeed."

Stahr is a symbol of intelligence and authority. Despite his background, he possesses a natural creative genius that has carried him "through trackless wastes of perception into fields where very few men were able to follow him." Moreover, he has the judgment and character of the capitalist men of action and the glamorous energy of the pioneer "builder of

LOVE AND MONEY: AN AMERICAN COMBINATION

Fitzgerald brought two innovations to American fiction, and in the way in which he developed them there is already a mark of his "Americanism." The theme of love is of central interest. . . . The ambiguity and the complexity of love are never the object of analysis in American fiction, but rather a mere pretext for metaphysical explorations. In Fitzgerald, for the first time, we witness instead a profound interest for the theme as such, and a corresponding intensity of artistic realization: the end of a sentimental delusion in *This Side of Paradise*, its pathetic consequences in *The Beautiful and Damned*, its ruin and tragedy in *Gatsby* and *Tender Is the Night*, its instrumental role in *The Last Tycoon*. The love motive is always at the center of these stories, no longer as a pretext but as a catalytic agent in reality. In Edgar Allan Poe the love passion had been mainly an expedient for self-commiseration, in Melville and Hawthorne it was the starting point for complex "moralities" or for a breathless spiritual adventure, in James a stratagem for the application of intelligence, in the naturalistic writers a means of exposure and denunciation, and in Hemingway himself only a marginal motive—even in *A Farewell to Arms*. In Fitzgerald the experience of love—youthful and deceitful, mature and altruistic, barren and tormented, as the case may be—finds its artistic consecration and is brought to the foreground of the action.

At the same time, Fitzgerald was able to discover another fictional possibility provided by American reality—the possibility of artistic treatment offered by the leisure class and the very rich. And since his love stories are set in that social context, the theme of love is developed interdependently with the theme of money and wealth. Fitzgerald seems in fact to be one of the most perceptive and sensitive interpreters of the interdepen-

---

empires." Like the Romans (and the Fords and Rockefellers), he is not only a creator but a ruler of creators, an adapter of men and things for his own purposes. Kathleen considers him more a king than any of the European monarchs she has met. He is the last of the "merchant princes."

AN IDEAL—AND IDEALISTIC—CAPITALIST

Stahr, however, is not merely a symbol of power and wealth; he is the ideal capitalist. His artistic ability and, above all, his humanity make him the last of the individualists and a dence between money and love as fictional possibilities, and his attitude in this respect is basically in keeping with the attitude that so many American writers have taken even in different cultural or social contexts. A fictional connection between the two themes has quite often been the distinctive mark of a good number of American writers since the very beginning of American literature, and it reflects a deeply rooted awareness of the close links between these two modes of experience. . . .

An "economic conscience" more than anything else is the distinguishing trait of Benjamin Franklin, and it is at the root of his *Autobiography*. Thoreau began *Walden* with a chapter on "Economy" and indulged every so often in careful reckonings. William Dean Howells sees love and money as opposing but interrelated principles in his bourgeois and genteel novels; Henry James has heroines and seducers revolve around fabulous inheritances. From Stephen Crane to Theodore Dreiser, a whole school of naturalistic writers saw money as a corrupting force and love as the only redeeming force. Dos Passos wrote a book on it *(The Big Money)*, and a whole series of proletarian writers with him, from Farrell to Steinbeck, exploited every possibility of the connection. Poe was aware of money as an obstacle to love or life; Pound regarded it as a determining factor of historical decadence and sexual sterility (Canto XLV); even Faulkner had Flem Snopes rise to financial predominance not only by cunning, but by a well-chosen rich partner. Fitzgerald wove his parables along the same lines, on the two themes of love and money, indissolubly connected. Thus, he linked himself with a traditional experience both human and cultural, but he also colored it with a residue of Puritan morality. Pressed by these two contrasting tensions, it is always the individual conscience that suffers in the dilemma.

Sergio Perosa, *The Art of F. Scott Fitzgerald*, 1965.

mourner for the golden age of capitalism. Stahr's compassion is his distinguishing characteristic. Like most brilliant men, "he had grown up dead cold," but resolved to learn "tolerance, kindness, forbearance, and even affection like lessons." As a paternalistic employer, he has inspired his employees to new heights of productivity and professional satisfaction. With a rare combination of idealism and practicality, he has resisted the pressures of economy and competition and has carried films "way up past the range and power of the theatre." Brimmer, the communist labor leader, fears his influence above all others because men like Stahr are the only heroic figures still capable of making capitalism attractive to the masses.

Yet Stahr's idealism is in the process of destroying him. Another cluster of images surrounding him suggests decay and death—the end of his reign. For some time before the novel opens, Stahr has been weakening physically; yet he works even harder, "ruling with a radiance that is almost moribund in its phosphorescence." Brimmer, at the climax of his debate with Stahr, realizes that the transferral of power is soon to come: "'Is *this* all? This frail half-sick person holding up the whole thing?'" The atmosphere of death hangs over all that Stahr does, and it is not the least of Fitzgerald's achievements that we feel that the old Hollywood and an era in American history are dying with him.

A FIGHT TO THE FINISH

Brimmer and Brady represent what will replace Stahr, who is caught in the widening split between the collective forces of Capital and Labor. Brimmer is a relatively sympathetic character, "a Spencer Tracy type," as Celia describes him. Although he is dedicated to Stahr's downfall, he regrets that history must make them enemies. Brady, a more important figure, is the composite image of "Wall Street," the enormous, depersonalized concentration of capital that is driving the individual out of the marketplace and transforming the adventure of frontier enterprise into a cynical pursuit of corporate control. Brady symbolizes this loss of identity; he never confronts us directly, even in the most climactic scenes. Schwartz senses him only as impending doom, one of the Furies pursuing him for having made a fatal slip on the financial tightrope of Hollywood. Even his daughter, Celia, finds it difficult to visualize him as person, except in the most general terms:

> What did father look like? I couldn't describe him except for once in New York when I met him where I didn't expect to! I was aware of a bulky, middle-aged man who looked a little ashamed of himself, and I wished he'd move on—and then I saw he was father.

His rise to power has been an accident, a trading on the talents of others. He has little knowledge of film production and hasn't learned much about "the feel of America." He is an exploiter rather than a creator, a "shrewd and lucky" manipulator who is not "a passable man."

The contrast between Stahr and Brady, as in *Gatsby*, is most clearly expressed in their approaches to sex. Stahr's affair with Kathleen, whatever its eventual fate, is highly romantic, emphasizing the dying values of both her European and his American tradition. Brady's materialism, however, emerges when Celia stumbles onto Birdie Peters in her father's office closet—a mistress "stuffed . . . naked into a hole in the wall in the middle of a business day."

According to Fitzgerald's outline for the novel, Stahr and Brady were to destroy each other in a struggle for control of Hollywood and, symbolically, all of American industry. Stahr must lose his fight not only because individualism has been pushed into the past by the corporations and the labor unions but also because the prize he seeks no longer exists in its original form. Stahr's affair with Kathleen fails because he must compare her with the lost perfection of his dead wife. And just as Kathleen (who "doesn't fit in with the grandeur Stahr demands of life") is a less glamorous copy of the woman who shared Stahr's days of glory, modern Hollywood is a pale imitation of its heroic frontier days—no longer worthy of his effort. In Fitzgerald's later work, Hollywood represents the totality of past and present. It is the last memory of the epic age of capitalism, and its surrender to the forces of collectivism, both in management and labor, will inevitably bury the magnificence of the past in the mediocrity of the present.

TRYING TO RECONCILE THE CONTRADICTION

The Last Tycoon is Fitzgerald's final version of the capitalist fable. Many critics have noted the real or imagined debt that this vision owes to Frederick Jackson Turner's interpretation of American history. An insistence on this dependence, however, presumes that Fitzgerald is attacking the Gospel of Wealth in an industrial age in the name of an earlier, agrarian America. Certainly he regrets the passing of individualism and the degradation of frontier democracy. But as we have seen, the dream of success permeates *The Great Gatsby* and *The Last Tycoon*. In these works, Fitzgerald attempts to reconcile the contradiction between the heroic ideal of individualism and the monster of greed and tyranny it must become. If he does not regret the passing of men like Carnegie and Rockefeller, he recognizes the immense scale on which they were reconstructing the New

World. And he laments for a world which could turn Gatsby's daily schedule into a formula for achievement—"a lavish, romantic past that perhaps will not come again into our time." Hollywood, for all its vulgarity, contained the vitality of that past. The tragedy in *The Last Tycoon*, as in *The Great Gatsby*, depends as much on the intensity of the hero's hope as on the finality of its disillusionment.

The Writers of the Twenties

John W. Aldridge

Literary critic and essayist John W. Aldridge discusses whether the writers of the 1920s—specifically those who spent at least part of that decade in Europe (Fitzgerald, Ernest Hemingway, Thomas Wolfe)—actually produced a rebirth of American literature, as many observers claim. Aldridge reexamines their work to find that most of these writers narrowly focused on a single subject: their own youth. Aldridge grants that they produced some of the freshest, most appealing literature in American literary history, but maintains that most failed to develop their themes sufficiently to qualify as a "rebirth" of literature. Aldridge, a frequent contributor of essays to the *New York Times Book Review, Saturday Review,* and *Harper's Magazine,* has written and edited several books on twentieth-century American literature, including *After the Lost Generation.*

The publication back in 1973 of Malcolm Cowley's *A Second Flowering* reopened once again a question most of us might have preferred to leave closed and may have assumed was long closed. Yet even today it continues to preoccupy us like the puzzle of some ancient unsolved crime, and the occasion of this essay may make it appropriate to explore some of its implications still further. Just how important, really, was the generation of writers who are commonly assumed to have produced a renascence of American literature in the twenties; what is the meaning and value of their contribution in the perspective of all that we know about them and all that has happened in our literature since their time?

Mr. Cowley, having spent more than fifty years studying these writers, may be forgiven if, at seventy-five, he was un-

Reprinted from *Classics & Contemporaries* by John W. Aldridge, by permission of the University of Missouri Press. Copyright © 1992 by the Curators of the University of Missouri.

able or unwilling to offer much more than a reiteration of opinions that over the years have grown habitual with him and have come to represent the official establishment answer to this question. His understandably strong feelings of proprietorship toward the twenties writers have caused him to take it for granted that, in spite of individual shortcomings of which he is well aware, they were, on the whole, the most distinguished literary generation the century has so far produced—the most distinguished, in fact, since the great first flowering of American literary talent in the generation of Emerson and Thoreau. Mr. Cowley has written eloquently in support of his position, and one can scarcely fault him for taking it. He has had a long career as a highly influential critical spokesman for these writers, most of whom were his personal friends. He was on the scene in Paris during the time when they were doing some of their best work, and he was one of the first critics to understand and in *Exile's Return* to explore the significance of the whole artistic phenomenon that so profoundly affected the character of our literature after the first World War. If anyone has earned the right to his biases, Mr. Cowley surely has.

For the rest of us the problem of coming to terms with the twenties writers is considerably more complex. We have existed for years in a state of gross informational surfeit, in which we have become so drugged and bored with knowledge concerning every aspect of their lives and works that the possibility of making new and original assessments of them must strike us as being very remote indeed. Furthermore, their achievement as artists is now effectively inseparable in our minds from the legendry of their lives, and their works are so commonly seen as sourcebooks of gossip and invitations to nostalgia that no balanced view of their literary merits can be maintained for long.

THE ONLY *REAL* WRITERS

Many of us also have to contend with our own emotional relation to these writers, a relation that cannot be as intimate and avuncular as Mr. Cowley's but is no less affected by sentiment or what, in the case of literary people younger than he, has so often been the most abject kind of filial admiration. After all, the twenties generation were once our very special and personal property. We came to love them long before it became official wisdom to do so, and there are complex loy-

alties that bind us equally to them and to that part of ourselves that was formed by their influence. For many of us
who discovered them at the right (or perhaps exactly the
wrong) age, they seemed quite simply the only *real* writers
there were, and so they became our proxy writers. They had
all the experiences we would have liked to have, and they
wrote exactly the books we wished we might have written. It
could be fairly said that they were the first and perhaps the
only generation of writers to capture our imaginations and to
dramatize an image of the literary life with which we could
identify because it combined creative achievement with the
freedom to explore the fullest possibilities of feeling and
being. We may have had the greatest respect for the work of
such older men as Dreiser, Mencken, Anderson, and Lewis,
but we did not envy them their lives. Their generation
seemed grey, remote, and eternally middle-aged. There was
something about them that smelled of beer, cigars, pool halls,
and the heavy sweat of craft and naturalism. One imagined
them going off to the office every morning—potbellied busi-
nessmen of letters—carrying their inspiration in a lunch pail.
But the twenties writers were a very different breed—elegant,
aesthetic, temperamentally gifted rather than soberly skilled,
as extravagant and wasteful as young British lords, yet profoundly self-preserving in their function as writers. They
were distinguished from their elders, above all, by their dedication to the Flaubertian ideal of the artist, their sense of belonging to an aristocratic fraternity of talent. But they also believed in the interdependence of art and experience, the
necessity that literature partake of, even as it transformed to
suit its own purposes, the felt realities and passions of the individual life.

They thus embodied for us an adolescent ideal that is
deeply rooted in the American mythos but that, in recent
years, only Norman Mailer has been able to emulate with
any conviction, the ideal of the writer as poet-profligate, our
fantasy inheritance from the English and French Romantics
and the disciples of Walter Pater that for the first time among
the twenties writers became a practical model of conduct for
Americans. Hence, they found it possible to live the life of
sensation with great vigor and still live the life of literature
with great dedication and success. They were able to have it
both ways so splendidly, and they made such excellent use
of the opportunity, that some of us will probably never man-

age to see them except against the high coloration of jealousy or adoration.

Another factor obscuring our view of these writers is that they were largely responsible for developing in us the standards by which we might have been able to judge them. For it was on the evidence of their work and that of their European contemporaries that we formed our first impressions of what literary effects were possible to the modern sensibility. No other standards derived from other historical periods seemed quite applicable to them, if only because so much of their significance resulted from their collective belief that they had outmoded the past by confronting a new reality in ways wholly unique to it and to them. Also, in a very real sense, the twenties writers provided the basic assumptions through which we came to perceive, and some of us to express, the experience of the modern world. Their works for a very long time seemed to have done all our essential imagining for us, just as they themselves seemed to have done our essential living, so that we had very little sense of being engaged with life that was not in some way connected with the profoundly seductive images of life with which they first came to dominate our imaginations.

JUNIOR DECADE ABROAD

As a result, our view of the literary life of the twenties is a complex mixture of myth and reality, of reality fantasized into myth and myth personalized to the point where it seems like something we ourselves experienced. One does not know, for example, whether the literature created the fantasy or the fantasy found its embodiment in the literary life. But surely a strong attraction of the period for young people was and may still be the fact that it represents their vision of the perfect college literary apprenticeship exported to Paris and prolonged for a decade. The intense, free life of Montparnasse was the idealized equivalent of the intense, free life of the campus literati. There in Paris, happily far away from parents and hometown, it was possible to get drunk as often as one pleased, to stay up all night making love, wander the streets howling into the dawn, be eternally young, sensitive, and promising, do all kinds of experimental work and publish it in the little magazines, be read by an audience of friends who were the perfect classmates, all people of brilliant talent and wit and yet, except for a few, remarkably kind and helpful about one's own work. There too one could enjoy the presence of older teachers and mentors like Pound, Anderson, and Stein, the quintessential writing instructors who were the first to recognize one's gifts and who gave so generously of their advice and encouragement. But perhaps even more important were certain other perquisites of these literary junior years abroad: The advantages of not having to hold down a job because checks were coming regularly from home or a fellowship, not having to be compromised by the bourgeois values of one's parents, not having to worry about marriage and a family, not having responsibilities of any kind except to Art, Truth, and Friendship.

It is not surprising that this image of the Paris literary life should have been embellished in our minds by a cast of personages, both fictional and actual, who have the clarity of outline, the individuality, and the emotional openness that, as a rule, only young people of college age seem to possess. Their appearance and behavior remain with us almost as if recollected from life or recorded in a class yearbook in which we seem to find versions of our own former selves. Nobody will ever be like them again, and nobody will need to be. For these people exist eternally in the roles fixed for them by memory and sentiment—larger than life because they belong to a generation that managed to mythologize its experience while still engaged in the act of having it.

There is the young Jay Gatsby, helplessly in love with the rich and sophisticated sorority girl, holding out his arms to the green light at the end of her boat dock; Amory Blaine proclaiming his valedictory "I know myself but that is all"; Jake Barnes muttering through those bitter, bitter teeth the best line in the senior play, "Yes, isn't it pretty to think so"; Scott and Zelda, the most popular and beautiful couple on campus, behaving insufferably at parties, jumping fully clothed into the Plaza fountain; Hemingway, the most talented boy in the class, writing his first stories at a table in the Closerie des Lilas; good old Thomas Wolfe, a boy who never seemed to stop growing, getting very drunk, waving his arms, and knocking out the electrical system of an entire town. And we remember the others, the people like Harry Crosby, Slater Brown, William Bird, Robert McAlmon, and the Gerald Murphys, who matter only because they were friends of the famous and now belong to history simply because everyone connected, however remotely, with the Paris literary life in the twenties now belongs to history.

The writers whom Leslie Fiedler once called "great stereotype-mongers" have bequeathed us themselves and their characters as clichés, and criticism has made more clichés out of the essential arguments that can be brought against them. Yet the most familiar argument is also the least avoidable. They were a group of highly talented but narrow writers, and their narrowness was most dramatically revealed in the fact that they had one abiding interest—themselves when young, an interest that, in the case of some of them, became the literary preoccupation of a lifetime. Their books had all the attributes of young consciousness. They were lyrical, nostalgic, sentimental, stylish, experimental, and iconoclastic, and they told over and over again the story of self-discovery through the first conquest of experience. We learned from them what it is like to grow up in the small towns of America, how it feels to fall in love, have sex, get drunk, go to war, be an American in Europe and all for the first time—to be so hungry for life that you want to consume all the food, liquor, and women in the world, or to discover that the system created by adults is capitalistic and corrupt or hypocritical and dull.

ONLY THE YOUNG ARE TRULY HUMAN IN THEIR EYES

Fitzgerald wrote the story of young romance and riotous youth and, remarkably enough, became famous at twenty-four largely on the strength of the fact that he informed the older generation about just how badly the young really behaved. Hemingway's first and best materials were an adolescent's adventures in Europe, his initiation into the mystery cult of foreign sports, bullfighting and big-game hunting, the loss of his innocence through the death of his ideals and his love in European war. Dos Passos found his most dependable subject in the totalitarianism of social hierarchies, whether political, economic, or military, where the integrity of the young was destroyed or severely compromised and the artistic spirit was broken under the grinding pressures of the machine. There are very few people over forty in this literature, and when they do appear we can usually recognize them by their stigmata of physical ugliness, venality, and hypocrisy. Only the young are truly human. But then the young are doomed to be the victims of the old, to die in their

wars, to be tricked by their deceits, and ruined through se-
duction by their false gods.

It is logical that the qualities we remember most clearly in
this literature are those that impressed us when we ourselves were young—the marvelous intensity about people
and raw experience, the preoccupation with the self, with
love, sex, freedom, time, adventure, the irreverence toward
the world of the fathers, the disdain for the adult religion of
work, self-sacrifice, expediency, competition, and confor-
mity. It is also logical that so many of these writers were able
to function effectively only so long as they could keep alive
their youthful responses. A number did not live into middle
age. Some died romantically young, others like Fitzgerald
died old while still chronologically young. Of those who survived beyond fifty, almost all were engaged in reiterating the
experiences of their youth or continued, as did Hemingway,
to write out of a fading memory of emotional and intellectual premises established during the time of their first intense engagement of life.

They were, in fact, the first American literary generation
to make being young into both a style of life and a state of
grace. It is largely because of their influence that so many
Americans are unable to perceive experience except as
something that happens to one up to the age of thirty, or to
understand that life can on occasion be something other
than a process of losing the intensities one was once able to
feel. At the end of that fateful confrontation between Gatsby
and Tom Buchanan in the Plaza Hotel, Nick Carraway suddenly remembers that it is his thirtieth birthday—"Thirty—
the promise of a decade of loneliness, a thinning list of single men to know, a thinning briefcase of enthusiasm,
thinning hair." Read for the first time at the age of eighteen,
the passage seems one of the most poignant in the novel. But
then, perhaps years later, we may come to recognize that our
sympathies should go not to Nick but to Fitzgerald. It is *his*
limited vision of the possibilities of life that is exposed here,
even as it is this same limitation that makes Gatsby a convincing and pathetic character.

One reason of course for this preoccupation with youth is
that the first world war had the effect of seeming to annihi-
late past history and the old styles of history. Hence, the generation that had fought in the war felt urgently the need to
establish new premises, to redefine the terms of existence.

Not only was this necessarily a task for youth, but it placed unique and dramatic emphasis on the responses of youth. Only the young were sensitive and adjustable enough to be able to determine whether a given emotion or experience conformed to the new standards of authenticity produced, at least in large part, by the war. Besides, they were the ones who had "been there," been initiated, had heard all the big words and learned that those words did not describe how they felt or what they had been through. Thus, the literature of the twenties is not merely a narcissistic but—as the example of Hemingway makes particularly clear—a testing literature, one in which the effort again and again is to create an accurate new idiom and at the same time to determine the truth or falsity of a radically new, essentially foreign experience—most often according to the responses of a provisional and existential, inevitably youthful self.

INNOCENCE AND PERSPECTIVE

Fortunately, there were elements that worked powerfully to the advantage of these writers. First, there was the fact that their consciousness of being unique and their experience unprecedented was validated by social and moral changes so profound that a literary career might be constructed around the process simply of recording them. These writers were in a position to be among the first to witness such changes, and they were aided greatly by what Frederick J. Hoffman once called their creatively "useful innocence," their small-town sensitivity to forms of conduct that, in spite of their surface sophistication, they could not help judging by the provincial standards they had been brought up on. It is not surprising that some of their best work has the incandescent quality of the astonished spectator, privileged to be on the scene of first encounters involving people who suddenly seem no longer to know by what assumptions they should behave.

Secondly, their prolonged apprenticeship in Europe enabled them to view American life from the perspective not only of distance but of adversary cultural values. They had inherited from their predecessors—most notably Lewis, Mencken, and Van Wyck Brooks—an intellectual arrogance, a disdain for bourgeois society, and a belief in the absolute supremacy of art and the artist that were formed into a metaphysics under the tutelage of Stein and Pound. They became cosmopolitan provincials abroad; they learned to judge

America by essentially elitist European standards; and of course they found America provincial. But since they were themselves provincial, their attitudes retained a dimension of ambivalence that helped to humanize their satire and finally made it seem an expression more of regret than contempt.

"Life Hasn't Much to Offer Except Youth"

It was, of course, Fitzgerald himself who served as his own most striking example of a person giving all he has to the first act's drama. The man who at twenty declared, "After all, life hasn't much to offer except youth and I suppose for older people the love of youth in others," wrote at forty-three to his wife, whose insanity paralleled his ill health, a visible sign of the wearing out:

> Twenty years ago *This Side of Paradise* was a best seller and we were settled in Westport. Ten years ago Paris was having almost its last great American season but we had quit the gay parade and you were gone to Switzerland. Five years ago I had my first bad stroke of illness and went to Asheville. Cards began falling badly for us much too early. The world has certainly caught up in the last four weeks. I hope the atmosphere in Montgomery is tranquil and not too full of war talk.

It is typical of Fitzgerald's outlook, a reflection both of his egotism and of his fine attunement to his time and place in history, to see the world catching up with the downward spiral of his private existence. For this devotee of Spengler, political, social, and personal elements merged at the given moment of composing his letter into the grand decline of the West.

Wendy Fairey, *Fitzgerald/Hemingway Annual 1979.*

They had, in short, a strong sense of belonging to, or being able to identify imaginatively with, place, perhaps just because they were physically so displaced—not only from home but from the past represented by home. They may have been creatively stimulated by the experience of living in a dramatic, radically changing present. But they could also feel anxious and uncertain and in need of the structures of coherence and identity they had left behind in the Midwest and South. This undoubtedly accounts for the fact that Hemingway and Fitzgerald were so continuously preoccupied with procedural questions, with the effort to formulate dependable rules of feeling and conduct. Hemingway's works can be read as a series of instruction manuals on how to respond to and behave in the testing situations of life now that the rules have changed and the world has become, in effect, an unknown foreign country. It might also be argued that some of his most dependable instructions are those he was able to reclaim from the past, in particular the American frontier past, the lessons of courage, fidelity, honor, and rectitude that might still have the power to influence human conduct when all other values were being called into question. Fitzgerald's best novels are restatements of Henry James's great theme: the implications of the misuse of power upon those who are innocent and helpless by those who are strong and unscrupulous.

In short, one finds in these writers and in some of their contemporaries a concern with the moral authenticity of certain traditions they might have presumed to be outmoded. It may be expressed only in a nostalgic recurrence to the locales that provided security in childhood—Hemingway's Big Two-Hearted River or Wolfe's Old Catawba. But it may also involve complex loyalties and codes of honor that once gave a human dimension to life—as Nick Carraway discovers through the experience of Gatsby, and Dick Diver through his marriage to Nicole. Both men derived a "sense of the fundamental decencies" from their fathers and so can evaluate and ultimately condemn a society in which such decencies no longer have meaning.

One of the very best of Fitzgerald's stories, "Babylon Revisited," is yet another expression of the desire to reconstitute certain values of moral discipline and self-control after the violent dissipations of the decade that ended in bankruptcy in 1929. Charlie Wales, a battered survivor of the time, returns to Paris in the hope of regaining custody of his daughter. To do this, he must prove to his sister-in-law that he has become a fit and responsible person. He very nearly succeeds in convincing her, but fails at the last moment when two of his old drinking friends reappear and destroy his chances of making a new life. Just as Nick after Gatsby's death wanted "the world to be in uniform and at a sort of moral attention forever," so Charlie felt the need "to jump back a whole generation and trust in character again as the eternally valuable element." But there is no escape from the consequences of his wasted past:

> Again the memory of those days swept over him like a nightmare—the people they had met traveling, the people who

couldn't add a row of figures or speak a coherent sentence . . .
the women and girls carried screaming with drink or drugs
out of public places—
    —The men who locked their wives out in the snow, be-
cause the snow of twenty-nine wasn't real snow. If you didn't
want it to be snow, you just paid some money.

The act of moral reclamation may be a necessity for every
literary generation. In America we do not so much build on
tradition as steal from it those elements we think may help
us to understand the always unprecedented experience of
our own time. The twenties writers had a singular relation
to the problem. They had the strongest sense that their experience was indeed unprecedented, and that the older
modes of literary statement were inadequate to describe it.
They therefore became excessively preoccupied with their
own experience and, in both their writing and their lives,
with the innovative and defiant. For reasons of temperament
and historical position many became fixated permanently at
the level of rite de passage where they were condemned forever to play the roles of rebellious sons and wayward daughters, able to find their identity only in the degree of their opposition to the literary and social conventions of the past.

Transcending the Adversarial Stance

Yet in reviewing their achievement one is struck by how
often their most admirable qualities seem to have been revealed at those rare moments when the writer was able, perhaps by accident, perhaps out of desperation, to transcend
the limits of the adversarial stance and define his materials
in some clear relation to the sustaining values of an older
moral tradition or a newly created artistic convention based
on those values. If Fitzgerald and Hemingway experienced
such moments, as some of their best work, most notably *The
Great Gatsby* and *The Sun Also Rises,* would seem to indi-
cate, they did so only occasionally, in part because the life of
their own time absorbed them too completely, and they were
so rarely able to see that life in a consistently maintained
moral perspective. . . .

    The examples of Faulkner and, on a less exalted level,
Thornton Wilder should serve to remind us that there were
alternatives to the more fashionable positions taken by so
many of the twenties generation. There were alternatives *if*
one possessed, as Wilder did, an intellectual culture broad

enough to enable one to draw creatively on the best resources of the Western literary tradition, or *if* one had Faulkner's access to the abundant resources of the southern tradition. But without these advantages, supplemented by talent of very large size, too many of the twenties writers remained locked into their first youthful responses to an experience that was too overwhelmingly intense to serve as very much more than the material of an often brilliant but very personal and limited literature. They may be forever established in our minds as the immensely charismatic personages of one of the most dramatic decades in our literary history. But it is significant that we can never separate them from the image we retain of the life of their time, just as they were unable, except at rare moments, to separate themselves, and in so doing, become larger than their experience, its imaginative possessors and masters, the shapers of those truths it contained that might have made timeless in art what is otherwise lost to history.

CHAPTER 2

The Great Gatsby

READINGS ON

F. SCOTT FITZGERALD

The Real Subject of *The Great Gatsby*

Arthur Mizener

Arthur Mizener has written extensively about Fitzgerald, including *The Far Side of Paradise* and *Scott Fitzgerald and His World*. Mizener writes that *The Great Gatsby* presents Fitzgerald's view of the most important moral choice a person can face: whether to live a life of virtue and moral discrimination or squander wealth on physical pleasures and abuse power. Fitzgerald feels that this choice is especially difficult for the wealthy, who have the means to choose either path. The various choices the characters in *Gatsby* make and the significance and consequences of those choices are, Mizener is convinced, the real subject of the book.

A few short years before he died—in 1936, to be exact—Scott Fitzgerald remarked that he had at last given up the idea by which he had lived his life. I think he had not really given it up, for if he had, he would have literally died then, as did Jay Gatsby in the same circumstances. But he believed he had. He described this idea as

> the old dream of being an entire man in the Goethe-Byron-Shaw tradition, with an opulent American touch, a sort of combination of J. P. Morgan, Topham Beauclerk and St. Francis of Assisi.

Feeling this way, he inevitably looked for a *realization* of his inner vision of the possibilities of life; and it seemed self-evident to him that only the rich and successful people in any society have the means and therefore the opportunity to make of life what it is possible for Topham Beauclerk and St. Francis of Assisi to imagine its being.

As a result of looking at the life he knew—American life, that is—in this way, he gradually developed a subtle and fas-

From "F. Scott Fitzgerald: *The Great Gatsby*" by Arthur Mizener, in *The American Novel: from James Fenimore Cooper to William Faulkner*, edited by Wallace Stegner. Copyright © 1965 by Basic Books, Inc. Reprinted by permission of BasicBooks, a division of HarperCollins Publishers, Inc.

cinating perception of the immensely complex relations between the ability that makes it possible for a man to get to the top in a competitive society and the ability that equips a man to conceive the "Good Life," between the talent for accumulation and the gift of imagination. The gift of imagination was, he knew, vital; no man could visualize the Good Life without it. But wealth, he saw, was important, too—not for itself, but because wealth alone makes it possible for a man actually to live the life the imagination conceives.

The most famous of all anecdotes about Fitzgerald concerns wealth. According to this anecdote, Fitzgerald once said to Hemingway, "The rich are different from you and me," and Hemingway replied, "Yes, they have more money." This exchange never actually took place; Hemingway invented it for a story called "The Snows of Kilimanjaro." But the remark Hemingway ascribes to Fitzgerald is a sentence from one of Fitzgerald's short stories called "The Rich Boy," a brilliant study of the special character of the very wealthy in America. Of Fitzgerald's sentence Lionel Trilling has said, in contrast to Hemingway, that "for this remark alone Fitzgerald is in Balzac's bosom in the heaven of all novelists."

For the rich who made the most of their unique opportunity to live the life of virtue with the maximum imaginative intensity, Fitzgerald felt something like hero worship. For the merely rich, those who did not use their wealth as a means to such a life, he felt the utmost contempt, what he once referred to as "the smouldering hatred of the peasant." He was convinced that the most important moral choice a man could face existed in its most fully developed form among the rich—the real, achievable choice between fineness of perception and of moral discrimination on the one hand, and the brutality of unimaginative, irresponsible power on the other. That is why he thought the rich are different from you and me and why he thought any failure on their part to use their wealth well constituted a crime that you and I are never given an opportunity to commit. It was this crime for which he condemned Daisy and Tom Buchanan in *The Great Gatsby*. Nick Carraway says:

> They were careless people, Tom and Daisy—they smashed up things and creatures and then retreated back into their money or their vast carelessness, or whatever it was that kept them together, and let other people clean up the mess they had made.

It is a great tribute to Fitzgerald's imagination that, despite his disapproval of such people, he understood them. In the end, he makes us see, Tom Buchanan is wistful and pathetic. At their final meeting, Nick Carraway shakes hands with Tom, feeling "suddenly as though I were talking to a child," as indeed he is, for with Tom's passion for what he childishly imagines to be "scientific stuff" about white supremacy, his ludicrous and sincere sentimentality about "nice girls" like his wife and his string of coarse, energetic mistresses, he is a fully conceived case of the undeveloped imagination. Daisy is even sadder, a girl who had caught a glimpse of the great life but who lacked the courage to live it, someone who chose in the end to live the sophisticated life rather than the loving life.

REALIZING THE GOOD LIFE

This, then, is the real subject of *The Great Gatsby*—the opportunity wealth provides for the realization of the Good Life and the necessity for what Fitzgerald calls "a heightened sensitivity to the promises of life" if people are to imagine the Good Life clearly enough to understand what they have the opportunity to achieve. This subject Fitzgerald visualized with great intensity in *The Great Gatsby;* it governs every detail in the book. Henry James once remarked that the history of the English novel up to his time had been a paradise of the loose end. There are no loose ends in *The Great Gatsby.* This is not just a matter of structure, though the plot of Gatsby is managed with great skill and economy. The complicated series of misunderstandings that lead up to the death of Myrtle Wilson is handled with amazing ease; the parallel between Gatsby's love of Daisy and Nick Carraway's love of Jordan Baker is precise and unobtrusive; the facts of Gatsby's business career are so quietly worked in that we scarcely remember how we learned them. But the really convincing evidence of the imaginative pressure under which the novel was created is the way the smallest details reinforce its meaning.

For example, in the book's first scene, when Nick is at the Buchanans' for dinner, Daisy invents one of her characteristic fantastic jokes about the butler who, she says, had to leave his previous position because he was required to polish silver all day and the polish affected his nose. Eighty odd pages later, when Daisy arrives at Nick's to have tea with

Gatsby, Nick alludes to this joke. "Does the gasoline affect his nose?" he asks Daisy of the chauffeur, and Daisy says solemnly, "I don't think so. Why?"

Or, when Gatsby is giving Nick his cheap-magazine account of his life, he says that he has

> lived like a young rajah in all the capitals of Europe [and then gets the names wrong]—Paris, Venice, Rome—collecting jewels, chiefly rubies, hunting big game, painting a little.

Nick is disgusted by this patent lie, this picture of what he calls "a turbaned 'character' leaking sawdust at every pore as he pursues a tiger through the Bois de Boulogne." But fifty pages later he sees in Gatsby's bedroom a photograph of Gatsby standing beside Dan Cody on Cody's yacht, and finds himself on the verge of "ask[ing] Gatsby to see the rubies."

Or, when Nick has his last meeting with Tom Buchanan on Fifth Avenue, Tom leaves him to go "into a jewelry store to buy a pearl necklace—or perhaps only a pair of cuff buttons—rid of my provincial squeamishness forever." These particulars are not fortuitous. Tom's engagement present to Daisy had been "a string of pearls valued at three hundred and fifty thousand dollars," and when Daisy, after her brief rebellion, finally appeared for the bridal dinner, "the pearls were around her neck"—like a chain. As for the cuff buttons, Meyer Wolfsheim, the novel's other brutal sentimentalist, is inordinately proud of his cuff buttons. He insists on Nick's examining them carefully, and explains to him that they are the "finest specimens of human molars." Tom's pearls may be, conventionally speaking, in better taste, but their purpose is to demonstrate his ownership of Daisy—the only kind of possession he can really understand—an ownership quite as gruesome in its politer way as Wolfsheim's ownership of men.

A FINE DESIGN

This imaginative use of realistic detail is one of the clearest signs that an author's imagination is working with full intensity. Another is fineness of design, and the design of *The Great Gatsby* is skillfully made, too. At its center is Nick Carraway, the narrator. Nick comes from a small, provincial, stable city in the Middle West. He has gone to Yale and there becomes to some extent an Easterner, so that after the war he chooses to live in the charming, rootless, power-hungry society of Long Island, though he is far from understanding fully its character. "Everybody I knew [from Yale] was in the bond business," he says with a glimpse of what is wrong, "so I supposed it could support one more single man."

Nick is thus, in manner and in superficial feeling, an Easterner, but his moral roots, though he does not fully realize it until the end of the novel, are in the Middle West. In the book's first scene we see him responding without doubt to the charm of the Buchanan house and of Daisy, adrift like some informal Fragonard goddess in the "bright rosy-colored space" of its drawing room. It is a very hot evening, too hot for Daisy to struggle up off the sofa when Nick comes in, and Daisy makes one of her charming jokes by way of apology: "I'm p-p-paralyzed with happiness," she says to him.

SECRET SOCIETY, HIDDEN DEFECTS

Yet by dinner time Nick begins to sense something he is not quite comfortable with in the Buchanans, though he is Daisy's cousin and Tom's college friend. "You make me feel uncivilized, Daisy," he says at the dinner table. "Can't we talk about crops or something?"—which is what they would have done at home, in the Middle West. After dinner, when Daisy is telling him about Tom's mistress and about how sophisticated and disillusioned she is, this feeling becomes more serious,

> as though the entire evening had been a trick of some sort to extract a contributory emotion from me. I waited, and sure enough in a moment she looked at me with an absolute smirk on her lovely face, as if she had asserted her membership in a rather distinguished secret society to which she and Tom belonged.

This reference to a secret society is no doubt Fitzgerald's joke at Yale's expense, perfectly natural in the context, since Nick and Tom had belonged to the same secret senior society at Yale. But it is something more, too. What Tom and Daisy have in common with one another and with all the people like them in the book is their membership in the snobbish secret society of the rich who are incapable of living the fully imagined life. Out of ignorance or cowardice they substitute for that life a childish game in which superficial good taste takes the place of genuine responsiveness, "what all the most advanced people think" takes the place of responsible intelligence, and being in fashion takes the place of a seriously imagined purpose. In the end these bonds between Tom and Daisy are stronger than Daisy's love for Gatsby.

Thus the life of Daisy and Tom and their friends is made the image of a life exquisitely graceful on the surface, with a moral defect at its heart that is only slowly revealed to Nick. The Buchanans stand on one side of Nick, at first appealing strongly to his sense of the glamour of Eastern life and, as the book progresses, disturbing more and more seriously his Middle-Western sense of decency. So far as they are concerned, *The Great Gatsby* is a history of the slow but steady decline of Nick's admiration for them, as the full evil of their moral irresponsibility is revealed to him and he loses interest in their glamour. Finally, he can no more accept Daisy's continuing to live with Tom than he can accept Wolfsheim's fixing the World Series of 1919. Daisy says of Tom's philandering, "You see I think everything's terrible anyhow. Everybody thinks so—the most advanced people." But on the whole she is rather proud of being a part of that everything. Nick's instinct, as he says, is to call for the police, just as that was his instinct when he learned that Wolfsheim had played "with the faith of fifty million people—with the single-mindedness of a burglar blowing a safe."

GATSBY

On the other side of Nick stands Gatsby, the son of a poor Minnesota farmer named James Gatz. Having fallen in love with Daisy when he was in training camp near Louisville, he sets out after the war to become as rich and gentlemanly as Tom so that he will be worthy to ask Daisy to leave Tom and marry him. In the simplest and most naïve way possible, with no awareness of the corruption that underlies them but rather taking them as models of the cultivated and civilized life, he sets out to imitate the ways of wealthy people like the Buchanans. He buys expensive cars; he imports his clothes from England; he seeks out "interesting" people. He even purchases what Nick ironically calls an "ancestral home" just across the bay from the Buchanans'.

Here again we can see the wonderful, unobtrusive skill with which Fitzgerald uses realistic detail symbolically. Houses in *The Great Gatsby* are much richer in meaning than the book's more obvious symbols; this is perhaps most evident in the way the house in Louisville where Gatsby woos Daisy is charged for us with Gatsby's feelings. Houses are especially significant in the book for the way they emphasize the meanings inherent in its central design, which places Nick in the middle with Gatsby on one side of him and the Buchanans on the other.

Nick has grown up in the Middle West, in the "Carraway house in a city where dwellings are still called through decades by a family's name." The Carraway house was no doubt ugly and dull by the fashionable standards of Long Island, but it was genuinely "ancestral." Nick was at home there; but he is so little at home in his West Egg bungalow that he says he has become "an original settler" when someone asks him the way into the village. In contrast to the Carraway house, Gatsby's house next door to Nick's bungalow, "a colossal affair by any standards," is as innocently awful in its ostentation as his clothes and his car—a freshly constructed "factual imitation of some Hotel de Ville in Normandy." In this Cecil de Mille set Gatsby tries to realize his dream.

The Buchanans

The Buchanans' "cheerful red-and-white Georgian Colonial mansion," though much more sophisticated in taste, is quite as fake in its own way as Gatsby's mansion, and its owners are quite as temporary occupants: Tom Buchanan has just bought it from "Demaine, the oil man," and at the end of the story he and Daisy, departing, leave no address. Indeed, the only place in which Tom seems ever to have felt enough at home to grieve over its loss is the apartment in New York where he spent odd moments with Myrtle Wilson, a dwelling even more temporary than the house at East Egg.

The Buchanans' house, like their life, is not evidently ridiculous, as is Gatsby's, but both are essentially dead, as Gatsby's are not. The Buchanans hardly pretend not to drift "here and there unrestfully wherever people played polo and were rich together"; but Gatsby's house and his life, for all their bad taste, are given purpose and meaning by his Platonic concept of himself, by his dreams—at least until the end, when Daisy's betrayal destroys his dream and "perhaps he no longer cared." Even Daisy can see that the innocently tasteless appurtenances of wealth with which Gatsby surrounds himself are expressions of his heroic idealism; Gatsby climaxes the all-important tour of his house on which he takes Daisy by pouring out before her an endless profusion of very showy, though imported shirts; and suddenly Daisy bows her head on the pile and weeps.

What Nick discovers at the end—as perhaps Gatsby finally did, too—is that, however lacking it may be in glamour, the life lived in the "bored, sprawling, swollen towns beyond the Ohio" is the only real one he has ever known. Compared to that, the Long Island life that Gatsby lived in the service of his dream, that the Buchanans lived in the service of their restless sophistication, that even Nick, in his ignorance, lived for a while, is a fantasy. "I see it," Nick says at the end,

> as a night scene by El Greco: a hundred houses, at once conventional and grotesque, crouching under a sullen, overhanging sky and a lustreless moon. In the foreground four solemn men in dress suits are walking along the sidewalk with a stretcher on which lies a drunken woman in a white evening dress. Her hand, which dangles over the side, sparkles cold with jewels. Gravely the men turn in at a house—the wrong house. But no one knows the woman's name, and no one cares.

Because of the importance of the idealism behind Gatsby's apparently meretricious life, Fitzgerald twice has Nick make it explicit. Once he says:

> There was something gorgeous about [Gatsby], some heightened sensitivity to the promises of life. . . . This responsiveness . . . was an extraordinary gift for hope, a romantic readiness such as I have never found in any other person.

And again he says:

> The truth is that Jay Gatsby of West Egg, Long Island, sprang from his Platonic conception of himself. . . . [He found himself in a world] of a vast, vulgar, meretricious beauty. So he invented just the sort of Jay Gatsby that a seventeen-year-old [American] boy would be likely to invent, and to this conception he was faithful to the end.

The stress here is on two remarkable characteristics of Gatsby's life. The first is the purity and intensity of Gatsby's desire to make real, in the actual world, an ideal mode of existence. The second is the way he is forced by the conditions of American society to use shoddy materials, to actualize his dream in the "vast, vulgar, meretricious beauty" which is all his world makes available to him.

NO IMPORTANT MORAL DISTINCTION

In a few short years after the war, Gatsby becomes as rich as Tom Buchanan by buying a chain of drugstores and using them as outlets for bootleg liquor and by organizing a large and efficient business for the disposal of stolen Liberty bonds. It is one of the fine incidental ironies of the novel that Gatsby has a first-rate executive talent and organizes large, profitable business enterprises with great skill, whereas Tom Buchanan inherits a huge fortune and never works at all. It is thus Gatsby, not Tom, who fulfills the conventional American ideal of conduct. It is true that Gatsby's businesses are illegal, and in the Plaza scene Tom attacks Gatsby with ostentatious piety as "a common swindler." But it is perfectly clear that Fitzgerald believes there is no important moral distinction between Gatsby's kind of business and any other. At one extreme of Fitzgerald's business community we have Wolfsheim and the West Egg people who attend Gatsby's parties; they are mostly in the movies, in politics, in gambling; they are able to grant the police commissioner frequent favors and have a good deal of influence; they are surrounded by an air of underworld notoriety. At the other extreme we have Tom Buchanan and the East Egg people; they play polo and watch their investments; they have a habit of authoritative arrogance to which everyone except their wives yields; they are socially prominent. But despite these superficial differences, these two worlds are fundamentally alike and are in fact interrelated. Both are morally and imaginatively infantile, and some of Tom's friends have invested in Gatsby's businesses. East Egg's manners are more refined than West Egg's, and less honest; that is the only real difference.

A PURE HEART

But the distinction that matters in *The Great Gatsby* does not depend on how people acquire their money: on that score Fitzgerald has serious doubts about everyone. It depends on how people use their wealth, and of all these people, only Gatsby, despite his bad taste, uses his money really well. In itself, for mere power or possession or self-indulgence, wealth means nothing to Gatsby; he is perfectly ready to throw it away—along with his life—when Daisy destroys his faith in her as the incarnation of his dream. Though Gatsby is, according to the law and Emily Post, a criminal and a fake, beneath his conventionally deplorable surface there is a purity of heart that gives every act of his life remarkable integrity. "No—Gatsby turned out all right at the end." So far as Gatsby is concerned, then, *The Great Gatsby* is a history of the rise of Nick's admiration for him, as the full, imaginative splendor of his purpose is slowly revealed to Nick and he ceases to care about Gatsby's superficial absurdity.

This is the essential design of *The Great Gatsby*, with Nick in the middle, torn between the superficial social grace and the unimaginative brutality of the wealthy and the imaginative intensity and moral idealism of the socially absurd and legally culpable self-made man. At the beginning of the book, Nick is charmed by Daisy and disgusted by Gatsby, who is, as an Eastern gentleman, so obviously a fake. At the end of the book he knows, as he calls out to Gatsby when he leaves him for the last time, that "They're a rotten crowd. You're worth the whole damned bunch put together."

> His gorgeous pink rag of a suit made a bright spot of color against the white steps, and I thought of the night when I first came to his ancestral home, three months before. The lawn and drive had been crowded with the faces of those who guessed at his corruption—and he had stood on those steps, concealing his incorruptible dream, as he waved them good-bye.

A Peculiarly American Attitude

Gatsby is Fitzgerald's most brilliant image of his deepest conviction, the conviction that life untouched by imagination is brutal and intolerable and that the imagined life must be made actual in the world if a man is to become anything more than a self-indulgent daydreamer. It is, I believe, a peculiarly American attitude. Americans are no doubt proud of their wealth and of the enterprise that is at least in part responsible for it. But they are seldom content with a merely material life; that kind of life seems to them, as Gatsby's life seemed to him after he lost faith in Daisy, material without being real. Only when it is animated by an ideal purpose does it seem real to them. This is, in fact, what we mean by "The American Dream," insofar as that dream is something possessed by each of us individually.

Fitzgerald was perfectly aware that Gatsby is representative in this way, and in the last page of the novel he firmly relates Gatsby's personal dream to the dream that has haunted American history from its beginning. Nick Carraway is sitting on the shore of Long Island back of Gatsby's now deserted house,

> And as the moon rose higher, the inessential houses began to melt away until gradually I became aware of the old island here that flowered once for Dutch sailors' eyes—a fresh, green breast of the new world. Its vanished trees, the trees that had made way for Gatsby's house, had once pandered in whispers to the last and greatest of all human dreams; for a transitory, enchanted moment man must have held his breath in the presence of this continent, compelled into an aesthetic contemplation he neither understood nor desired, face to face for the last time in history with something commensurate with his capacity for wonder.

> And as I sat there brooding on the old, unknown world, I thought of Gatsby. . . .

T. S. Eliot once called *The Great Gatsby* "the first step in American fiction since Henry James," for in it Fitzgerald realized, for the first time in twentieth-century terms, James's understanding of the dramatic conflict between good and evil that is inherent in American life.

Fitzgerald's Sense of Ambiguity

C.W.E. Bigsby

Many critics see in Fitzgerald's work a stark comparison of various dualities—wealth and poverty, purity and corruption. According to C.W.E. Bigsby, a senior lecturer in American literature at the University of East Anglia in England, however, by the time Fitzgerald wrote *The Great Gatsby*, he no longer believed the world was divided so neatly into areas of black and white. Instead, Bigsby believes, *Gatsby* reflects Fitzgerald's maturing recognition of the ambiguities inherent in the choices that must be made in the real world.

In *The Liberal Imagination* Lionel Trilling points out that 'in any culture there are likely to be certain artists who contain a large part of the dialectic within themselves . . . the very essence . . . the yes and no of their culture'. This was especially true of F. Scott Fitzgerald, who confessed, in one of his *Esquire* pieces, that he could never understand why he had come to be identified with the objects of his horror. The truth was that, at least in his early years as a writer, he squandered his talent in order to finance the very excesses against which his puritanical soul rebelled. While he denounced a period which had little time for those not in a position to enjoy the joke, those who—like the three hungry men in Hart Crane's 'The Bridge'—are left behind by the glaring rush of the 'Twentieth Century', he was fatally attracted by the very thing he sought to expose. Rather like Amory Blaine, in his first novel, he felt that 'it isn't that I mind the glittering caste system . . . but gosh . . . I've got to be one of them.' As he acquired greater wealth so he compensated by adopting a romantic radicalism which never got much beyond a vague conviction that wealth, like beauty, was in some way associated with

evil, and which anyway never found its way into his work as
a force to counter the bland materialism which he identified
around him. The conversion of the protagonist of *This Side
of Paradise* to a naïve socialism had had less to do with genuine political persuasion than with Fitzgerald's sense of a
universe which polarized around wealth and poverty, purity
and corruption, youth and age. Yet, with *The Great Gatsby*
and later with *Tender Is the Night* and *The Last Tycoon,* he did
begin to appreciate the creative tensions within his own
work, to admire 'the ability to hold two opposed ideas in the
mind at the same time, and still retain the ability to function'
[Fitzgerald, *The Crack-Up and Other Pieces and Stories*]. If he
never fully understood the precise nature of this dialectic he
did sense the essential dilemmas of his age in a more profound way than his early fashionable success might have
suggested. He began, with *The Great Gatsby,* to retreat from
the manichean[1] sensibility of his early work, to acknowledge
a crucial ambiguity at the heart of human affairs and to re-
ject the casual moral assumptions of his first two novels. He
also began to delineate with greater care and perception the
line which links the individual with the body politic, to see
on a more fundamental level the connection between personal and public history. . . .

A New Vision and Dedication

The Great Gatsby came at a time when Fitzgerald's popularity was on the wane. His role as the main spokesman for his
generation had been taken over by John Dos Passos and Sinclair Lewis, while his own early success was proving a
two-edged weapon; he was increasingly associated with an
era which was already considered passé. Allied with this was
Fitzgerald's sense of his own deterioration since his comple-
tion of *The Beautiful and Damned.* *The Great Gatsby,* therefore, was to be not merely an attempt to re-establish his ascendancy, with the critics as well as with a fickle public, but
also an assertion of his own confidence and integrity. It was
to be a victory of the will as much as an artistic achievement.

Henry Dan Piper and others have traced the changing literary influences at work on Fitzgerald at this time, especially the significance of James and Conrad. Whatever the
effect of these influences, it is certainly true that Fitzgerald

---

1. dualistic; characterized by two eternal, opposing principles, as good and evil

approached this work with a care which had scarcely marked his earlier novels. As the author [Fitzgerald] remarked, 'Never before did one try to keep his conscience as pure.' To John Aldridge, writing in 1951, the achievement of *Gatsby* derived from the fact that it was written 'during that fragile moment when the drive of youth meets with the intuitive wisdom of first maturity, and before either the diseases of youth or the waverings of age begin to show through'. While this somewhat naïve concept of balance has its attractions, as a general principle it would seem to have rather limited application. However, Fitzgerald's age was certainly important in one respect at least. Although we are told that he kept Ginevra King's[2] letters, even having them bound into a book, he was now able to regard his own youth with a degree of detachment not evidenced before. Hence, that uncritical attitude towards nostalgia and poignancy which had dominated *This Side of Paradise* and *The Beautiful and Damned* is abandoned in favour of a more complex and ambiguous response. He now succeeds in detailing emotional response without succumbing to it. He recognizes the limitations of sentiment, and sees his personal dreams as part of a larger illusion. Thus his obsession with lost youth becomes a national concern with squandered innocence and unfulfilled aspirations. Whether this was a result of 'the intuitive wisdom of first maturity' rather than a hard-earned insight derived from his own bitter experience it is impossible to say, but nevertheless it was the combination of this new vision and his own dedication to craft which resulted in the subtle nuances of *The Great Gatsby*.

An Unrecognized Ambiguity

The full extent of Fitzgerald's acknowledgment of ambiguity has never really been appreciated. Critics, swayed perhaps by the moral absolutes of his earlier work, have constantly been tempted to impose on this novel precisely that manichean tendency which he was attacking and from which he was struggling to escape. The contrast between city and country is apparently so deeply engrained in American sensibility that Fitzgerald's ambivalent attitude passes largely unremarked.

For Arthur Mizener, '*The Great Gatsby* becomes a kind of tragic pastoral, with the East the exemplar of urban sophisti-

---

2. Fitzgerald fell in love with King while he was in college; she did not return his affection.

cation and culture and corruption, and the West, "the bored, sprawling, swollen towns beyond the Ohio", the exemplar of simple virtue.' To Sergio Perosa, similarly, the novel is concerned with 'the typical American myth of the geographic and moral juxtaposition between the two poles of the nation to which a symbolic meaning is attached: the innocence of the flowering fields of wheat, the corruption and sterility of the city.' But the West has long since been corrupted by the forebears of Buchanan, Gatsby and even Carraway. Nick comes not from some agrarian hinterland but from a town in which his family had won ascendancy as the result of a great uncle who had sent a substitute to the Civil War (Grover Cleveland's particular sin) and himself founded a hardware business. Buchanan's careless wealth derives direct from the Mid-West as does Gatsby's amorality. Indeed, it is perhaps significant that the latter's childhood Horatio Alger principles for attaining wealth and personal success had been inscribed in a copy of *Hopalong Cassidy*. The American dream flourished in the West and the prime representative of this code, appropriately enough, is Dan Cody, 'the pioneer debauchee, who during one phase of American life brought back to the Eastern seaboard the savage violence of the frontier brothel and saloon'. It is worth remembering, after all, that the action of Fitzgerald's bitter attack on ruthless capitalism, 'The Diamond as Big as the Ritz', takes place in the West and not amid the supposed corruptions of New York.

A Re-Enactment of the American Experience

Tom Buchanan, living in his mock-colonial mansion, seems in many ways to be a figure derived directly from the frontier. We are told, for example, that not even 'the effeminate swank of his riding clothes could hide the enormous power of that body—he seemed to fill those glistening boots until he strained the top lacing, and you could see a great pack of muscle shifting when his shoulder moved under his thin coat'. Buchanan is an exploiter. He is a careless man who 'smashed up things and creatures'. He is close kin to Devereux Warren in *Tender Is the Night* who, with his 'fine shoulders shaking with awful sobs inside his easy-fitting coat', sees innocence as a provocation. Fitzgerald explodes the old mythology and in *Tender Is the Night* denounces 'the illusions of eternal strength and health, and of the eternal goodness of people: illusions of a nation, the lies of generations of frontier mothers who had to croon falsely, that there were no wolves outside the cabin door.' The exchange of the old world for the new can no longer be looked on as the exchange of innocence for corruption or the substitution of the dream for a sordid reality. This was an ambivalence which had previously escaped him. Gatsby, the sun-burned attractive young man who had discovered that 'people liked him when he smiled', is thus an inheritor of an already tarnished dream. Having naturalized his alien-sounding name he pursues a romantic vision but does so in a country whose primal innocence has long since been destroyed. Gatsby's experience is in many ways a simple re-enactment of the American experience. He has lost 'the old warm world' and in return has inherited 'an unfamiliar sky through frightening leaves. . . . A new world, material without being real, where poor ghosts', like himself 'breathing dreams like air, drifted fortuitously about'.

Yet, while Fitzgerald is at pains to avoid the simple polarity which Mizener identifies he does draw heavily on the usual images of east and west. East and West Egg in some ways present a microcosm of this situation. Yet, once again, despite Nick's remark that there is a 'bizarre and not a little sinister contrast' between the two communities, their differences are more apparent than real. They are both composed of essentially the same forces, as Fitzgerald makes plain in his Whitmanesque list of their inhabitants. West Egg may demonstrate a 'raw vigour' that chafes 'under the old euphemisms' but it is distinguished from East Egg only in the degree of its soulless wealth. While the East has the 'quality of distortion' and occupies the physical centre of the novel, this, as Nick finally realizes, had been 'a story of the West, after all'. The reductive irony of Nick's retreat to the corrupt Mid-West at the end of the novel depends, of course, precisely on our acceptance of the integrity of America's central myth.

THE IMAGE OF HIS DOUBLE VISION

But if the West provides evidence of Fitzgerald's new sense of ambiguity, the city too is in many ways the image of his double vision. He is at once attracted and repelled by what he sees. It represents corruption and graft but, with its towering white buildings, it seems to contain the essence of that pure dream of national and self-fulfillment. As he wrote in 'My Lost City', 'New York had all the irridesence of the beginning

of the world', yet whole sections 'had grown rather poiso-
nous'. Thus he must eventually leave the city which 'no
longer whispers of fantastic success and eternal youth', only
lamenting that 'I have lost my splendid mirage' and calling
out with mock romantic intonation, 'Come back, come back,
O glittering and white.' Daisy Buchanan, similarly associated
throughout with white, contains the same ambivalence and
as we penetrate the disguises of the one so we do those of the
other. Nothing is what it seems; innocence is merely an invitation to corruption, the historical process is irrevocable, pro-
grammatic categories are an illusion to be destroyed.

IDENTIFYING MORAL POLARITIES

Within the novel it is Nick Carraway who insists on identify-
ing moral polarities. It is with 'a sort of heady excitement'
that he imposes a radical simplicity on the people who sur-
round him. 'There are', he feels, 'only the pursued, the pursuing, the busy and the tired.' The real progress of the book
is thus Carraway's growing perception of the inadequacy of
such an attitude. His early conviction that 'Life is much
more successfully looked at from a single window' has to
bow before Gatsby's demonstration of the fallibility of such
a stance. In fact the reader's acknowledgment of the im-
morality of Nick's values and his unreliability as a neutral
observer is as crucial to an understanding of *The Great
Gatsby* as a similar appreciation is to an understanding of
The Turn of the Screw by Henry James.

Most of the contrasts in the book are more apparent than
real and Fitzgerald is at pains to link the experiences of Nick,
Gatsby, Tom, Daisy and the Wilsons until it is obvious that
they are all aspects of the same malaise. As Nick remarks,
'perhaps we possessed some deficiency in common'. In fact in
many ways the parallels between Gatsby and Tom Buchanan,
for example, are more important than the obvious diver-
gences. Like Tom, Gatsby 'took what he could get, ravenously
and unscrupulously'. Despite the romantic facade with
which he cloaks his relationship with Daisy it is no different
in kind to Tom's tawdry relationship with Myrtle Wilson.

A SOCIETY WITHOUT A MORAL CODE

This is a society lacking in moral responsibility and having
no ethical basis for action. The chain of motor accidents
which occur throughout the book merely provides evidence

of the carelessness with which the characters conduct their lives. Nor is it the Buchanans alone who show evidence of this irresponsibility. Jordan Baker, who lacks any kind of moral code, retreats into amused neutrality in the face of the crisis in her friends' lives. Fitzgerald's description of her as 'balancing something . . . which was quite likely to fall' is not merely an arbitrary device of characterization but an accurate image of her moral neutrality. The same is essentially true of Nick who, our sympathies notwithstanding, plays a morally ambiguous role in cooperating with Gatsby's adulterous schemes. As he plays pander to Gatsby's somewhat ponderous attempts at adultery he shares both the excitement and the tawdriness of his amoral pursuit of the ideal. He is by no means the innocent from the Mid-West to be contrasted with the corruption of the city dweller. A man determined to 'reserve all judgment' he attracts confidences and trust and yet responds to 'the secret griefs of wild, unknown men' with 'feigned sleep, preoccupation, or a hostile levity'. When at the height of the showdown at the hotel he suddenly remarks 'I just remembered that today's my birthday' his comment is an indication of his own self-absorption. In pursuit of their own fantasies individuals abandon moral considerations. As Fitzgerald himself wrote, 'That's the whole burden of this novel . . . the loss of those illusions that give such colour to the world that you don't care whether things are true or false so long as they partake of the magical glory.' On a more personal level this leads to the menacing disinterest of Jordan Baker and Nick Carraway, to the destructiveness of Daisy and Tom Buchanan, and to the sad corruption of Jay Gatsby. The point is not so much that the dream has been corrupted but rather that it always carried within it the seeds of its own corruption. As he wrote later in 'My Lost City', 'innocence is no end in itself'. In order to preserve his youthful vision of himself and of Daisy, Gatsby sells out to Wolfsheim and sees his adulterous advances as an attempt to rescue Daisy from a loveless marriage. He reshapes reality to fit his own delusions. But as a consequence he bears a direct responsibility both for his own death and for the death of Myrtle Wilson. In a sense, therefore, the deranged Mr. Wilson is right in singling out Gatsby for his revenge for, as one of Arthur Miller's characters remarks in 'After the Fall', to maintain our innocence we 'kill most easily'.

A Glorious, Futile Dream

Yet, despite his stringent analysis of the failure of the American dream, in a novel which was to have borne the significant title, *Under the Red White and Blue*, Fitzgerald cannot bring himself to denounce the embodiment of that vision. Even in the face of corruption and defeat there is an attraction in that man who can preserve his illusions intact. Like Willy Loman, Gatsby has all the wrong dreams but the single-mindedness, the spiritual integrity with which he pursues them, commands respect. It is perhaps to be expected that Fitzgerald, who wrote in a letter that 'like Gatsby I have only hope', would react ambiguously to Gatsby's vulgar yet curiously glorious quest. Gatsby simplifies his life by mortgaging himself to a single dominating obsession and though the novel demonstrates the danger of doing so Fitzgerald, who was tempted by the same strategy, could not condemn him. Like Nick Carraway, who was 'within and without, simultaneously enchanted and repelled by the inexhaustible variety of life'; he and his hero contain the 'yes and the no' of their culture without fully appreciating the conflict between historical process and animating myth.

The Danger of Romantic Promise

Gatsby does become a kind of hero. His wealth, though ill-gotten and squandered to little real purpose, nonetheless gives him a spurious stature, even in Fitzgerald's eyes. But surely the defeat of Gatsby finally signifies little but the demise of a kind of futile romanticism which had little to recommend itself anyway. If he represents anything beyond himself it is the impossibility of pursuing romantic dreams in an unromantic world and the emptiness of Horatio Alger promises. Carraway's action in rubbing out the obscenity scrawled on the steps of Gatsby's mansion is his attempt to preserve what he sees as the essential purity and innocence of the dead man, but not only is this innocence naïve and nonfunctional, it is also, as we have seen, dangerous. Fitzgerald never really confronts the paradox which he has constructed for himself, nor has he fully worked out his attitude towards the rich. Gatsby, after all, is corrupted not simply by money but by his naïve faith in the integrity and permanence of innocence, while the vulgarity of the rich Buchanans is matched by the crassness of the poor Myrtle

Wilson and her friends. The symbols of wealth, the motor car and the swimming pool, are certainly associated with death but so is the ash-landscape which surrounds the Wilson garage. Gatsby is betrayed not by wealth or the assumption that money can buy anything but by his belief that anything of value can survive the standards of the marketplace. In so far as his quest for a lost past is linked to the national mythology of New World innocence he has a symbolic dimension, but Fitzgerald's ambiguous response leaves the reader uncertain of the writer's view of the future.

Media in
The Great Gatsby

Ronald Berman

The Great Gatsby is permeated with images of—and from—visual media, from films and magazines to books and billboards, notes Ronald Berman, professor of literature at the University of California, San Diego. These images support the claim that society treats everything—consumer goods, people, even ideas—as commodities, things to be bought and sold. The images also mark Fitzgerald's experiment in visual writing; he uses techniques from still and movie photography to create scenes based on imagery rather than dialogue.

Gertrude Stein was interested in "how everybody is doing everything," a phrase that presupposes intense interest in things as disparate as intellectual style and everyday marketing. Miles Orvell covers both meanings in his cultural history of the early twentieth century, invoking the new "visual environment" of industrialism and its fascination for writers. Important elements were "photography, advertisements, and cinema," the modes of commercial image and print that affected and created style. These modes meant more, however, than the sale of commodities. Orvell cites Vachel Lindsay: "American civilization grows more hieroglyphic every day. The cartoons of Darling, the advertisements in the back of the magazines and on the billboards and in the streetcars, the acres of photographs in the Sunday newspapers, make us into a hieroglyphic civilization far nearer to Egypt than to England." One doesn't know about Egypt, but Lindsay does state part of Fitzgerald's repertory. Fitzgerald himself has become a reference point for "how everybody is doing everything." A recent survey of French fashion in the twenties by the Curator of Costume at the Museum of the City of New York, JoAnne Olian, begins by invoking his awareness of the new universal style. His statement about Paris—"everything that happened there seemed to have something to do with art"—seems to echo Gertrude Stein. We recall that Jordan Baker's name implies one kind of technology, and we may conclude that her appearance suggests another, as Olian observes: "Flattened, impossibly elongated figures attest to Cubist influence as well as that of Marie Laurencin and Modigliani. The asymmetry, geometrically precise pleats and tubular forms of dresses and figures relate directly to painting."

Marketplace relations are the other half of Fitzgerald's observation—and, I think, of Gertrude Stein's. . . .

MARKETPLACE RELATIONSHIPS

The marketplace of *The Great Gatsby* is located on Broadway, and the geography of the narrative encircles it, going south on Fifth Avenue to the borders of Murray Hill, then west to Pennsylvania Station, north to those big movies in the fifties, then east again to the Plaza. This area serves not only as the location for Nick's meeting with Wolfsheim, the beginning of his affair with Jordan, and the breakup of Gatsby's own affair with Daisy: Broadway contains the newsstands, movies, and theaters that offer ideas as commodities. The movies are probably most important. Movies sell not only styles but identities; and their effect is redoubled by the magazines and rotogravures and dailies that are the matrix of allusion in the text.

The language of the marketplace infiltrates everywhere. Wilson can't tell the difference between God and an advertisement; Nick sees Jordan for the last time, "thinking she looked like a good illustration." The tactic of placing the description so firmly in marketplace terms states silently the nature of relationship. Feelings and perceptions may even be provided by the marketplace. Marketplace relations dominate relations in the text. Myrtle buys her dog and Tom buys Myrtle. Nick rents, Gatsby buys, the Buchanans inherit. McKee, the idiot photographer who represents so much of the salesmanship in the narrative, lives to peddle his work on the North Shore. One moment in the text reverses the Jamesian theme of Americans abroad: "I was immediately struck by the number of young Englishmen dotted about; all well dressed, all looking a little hungry, and all talking in

low, earnest voices to solid and prosperous Americans. I was
sure that they were selling something: bonds or insurance
or automobiles." Commodities are definitions: Wilson
knows that Tom's car is the equivalent of his own going west
to start a new life; Gatsby knows that his gorgeous and
melodic car establishes his status.

THOSE EYES

*Seven months before Fitzgerald finished the manuscript
of* The Great Gatsby, *Max Perkins, his editor at Scribner's, commissioned artwork for the book jacket. Although
many editions of the book with a variety of cover art have
been published over the years, Scribner's used the original Art
Deco artwork again when it published a new edition in 1980.
The following is from Charles Scribner III's introduction to
that edition.*

Perkins . . . proceeded to commission an artist to paint the
dust jacket. An Art Deco tour de force, it portrays Daisy's
wide, brooding eyes (from one of which streams a lumines-
cent green tear) hovering over the festive, carnival-like lights
of New York City. Hemingway was later to describe it as the
ugliest jacket he'd ever seen, but Fitzgerald, writing from
France in the summer of 1924, insisted: "For Christ's sake
don't give anyone that jacket you're saving for me. *I've written
it into the book.*" [Italics mine.]

Thus the dominant symbol in the novel, the billboard eyes of
Dr. T. J. Eckleburg, owed its origins to the artist Francis Cugat.
I do not know of another case in which an author acknowledges so central a debt to an illustrator. This jacket, used on
the first edition, was recently revived for the Scribner Classics
edition of *Gatsby.* After half a century the highly stylized
image once again appears fresh and effective, and in vogue:
such are the cycles of taste.

Especially when Myrtle Wilson is involved in the action,
we can see what Fitzgerald has learned about the American
marketplace. When Myrtle assembles herself, complete to
dress, dog, apartment, and dialogue ("My Dear"), we see not
only her own vast energies but those of the economy and the
new consumer culture. Through Myrtle we become aware of
the realm of imitation, hence of the human dynamics of the
story. The party at Myrtle's apartment is one of the great
messes in literature. Yet everywhere among the fallen are

contravening images: "to move about was to stumble continually over scenes of ladies swinging in the gardens of Versailles." These scenes of the aristocracy of Fragonard, Boucher, Watteau, and Le Brun [French painters of the seventeenth and eighteenth centuries] belong now to manufactured interior decoration. They have been stamped out in their thousands. The subject may be French, but the technique is Hogarthian: the apartment is itself an economy, full of objects and commodities that have been duplicated. As his biographer Ronald Paulson says of Hogarth, "the real, feigned (acted), carved, and painted are all related within a single picture. The richness of literary content cannot be dissociated from the effect of the purely formal elements." In this case there are "scenes" within the scene that both parody and describe. The assembly-line tapestries state high life as Myrtle imagines it, fully clothed, richly at leisure, always dressed for a part. And they remind us, as objects and commodities and replications do throughout the text, that ideas are things.

IDEAL FORMS IN THE MEDIA

The characters of *The Great Gatsby* see ideal forms of themselves in film and in magazines. They are conscious, sometimes deeply and emotionally so, of advertisements. The narrative uses a highly intentional language of replication: "picture," "illustration," "advertisement," "photograph," "newspaper reports," "copy," and other things which continually argue that they are as "true" as Gatsby's photograph of Trinity Quad, and as "real" as his father's photograph of the great house on West Egg. But this language prepares us to understand also that how we do everything is theatrical. There is hardly a character in the novel who does not have an ideal self in mind, a self which is constructed or achieved. But the sense of self—even dreams of selfhood—in this story are the products of ideology or market enterprise. The idea of self is often specifically related to magazines and movies. People play at roles and sometimes even seem to have scripts in mind: there is Myrtle, who shows us in her apartment the way she looks after she has become what she thinks she is. We see Tom self-consciously wrapped in the robes of Native Americanism, ready, according to Nick Carraway, to pose for a painting of Civilization on the Barricades. There is Daisy playing always to an audience and, in one startling moment that links the rhetoric of film to text, viewed in front of the gorgeous, empty actress who is her simulacrum. But theatricality is not only a way of expressing desires but of concealing them. We are accustomed to think of *The Great Gatsby* as a story of mobility and change, but it is also a story of disguise, that is to say, of appearing to change while remaining the same.

BROADWAY VS. HOLLYWOOD

One of the most powerful oppositions in the book is that between Broadway and Hollywood. Both stand for artifice, but the former stands also for emotional authenticity. Gatsby may be "a regular Belasco" or producer of his own life's theater, but the "act" he puts on is considerably preferable to other kinds of acting and enactment. Daisy is drawn to the distancing, aesthetic and moral, of Hollywood—her genre, so to speak, is film, or at least film romance. Gatsby is a figure of Broadway, a place and an idea with an overwhelming presence in the text. Broadway sells dreams—and even ideologies—but it expresses real desires, calls on real feelings. It is where Gatsby comes back to life as Wolfsheim lifts him out of the street. It is where his guests come from in their "simplicity of heart" that corresponds to his own combination of vulgarity and emotional authenticity. It is Gatsby's milieu, and it becomes Nick's. Very little is emotionally or sexually disguised on Broadway.

Fitzgerald's feeling for the movie houses and poolrooms and restaurants and revues of midtown—he called it a "passion for Broadway"—corresponds to Edmund Wilson's. We see a self-conscious, explicit association between the two writers on this subject. According to Wilson, in 1923, the *Follies* "has in it something of Riverside Drive, of the Plaza, of Scott Fitzgerald's novels." There is, he says, "something wonderful about the *Follies*," and he is taken especially with its "vitality." Like Nick Carraway, Wilson finds himself "haunted" by the brassy, obscene music of city nights. Wilson discriminates, as Fitzgerald does, between the intensely rhythmic flow of music and the "harsh and complicated harmonies" of "nervous intensity" that the city betrays. Both writers associate dissonance with Broadway, and with the revelation of authenticity. But at Gatsby's second party Nick feels "many-colored, many-keyed commotion . . . a pervading harshness" that Daisy plainly does not want to understand.

In terms of technique, we will often see things, landscape and human objects, through the momentary glimpse of film and lens. The text will direct our attention to certain "scenes" by looking at them through the "flicker" of film movement—on Broadway, or crossing the Queensboro Bridge we see a mechanical world through mechanical means. When we look at Tom Buchanan, on our first assessment of him, he becomes for the moment a kind of machine in himself, and our perception of his bodily structure is in fact the perception by a moving-picture lens of an object in front of it. Nothing could be more appropriate than the inspection of one machine, calculated in terms of its force and leverage, by another.

STILL AND MOVING PICTURES

The text is permeated with references to still photography; film development, prints, copies, illustrations, etc. But some of its longest scenes depend on the audience's familiarity with "moving-picture" technique and technology. Possibly the most noticeable thing about such scenes is their silence. Part of Fitzgerald's experiment in this novel is the rendition of gesture that takes the place of speech. There is what seems to be intentional correspondence to the perception of the silent lens. There are certain silent scenes in *The Great Gatsby* that are, I think, openly cinematic, as in the theater view that we get of Tom and Daisy through the pantry window in which they are on stage in the light and we see them from the dark. Such scenes can be reminiscent of film staging, with special kinds of lighting and even props. Or they can suggest the perspective (and even the operation) of lenses. They will at times invoke the idiom of photography, as when expressions on Myrtle's face appear as if they were "objects" in "a slowly developing picture." In addition to film technique there is film allusion. At certain moments in the narrative we are intended to see Daisy and Myrtle through the new mythology (and vocabulary) of social character: Daisy loves to act out the script of the Poor Little Rich Girl while Myrtle echoes many of the social-climbing themes of movies about "working girls" who marry rich and Rise to the Top.

EXAMINING THE MEANING OF CHANGE

Fitzgerald has a particular strategy for the examination of the meaning of change. He rarely refers himself to history.

He had great difficulty, as the novel was composed, in dealing with Gatsby's biography. He clearly has little interest in politics—this is a novel in which parties and Congress and the great issues of the moment are invisible, except through Tom Buchanan's dim refraction of the politics of race and immigration. The novel's extraordinary grasp of change both personal and social is displayed through a different kind of allusion. The issue of change takes part of its definition from texts. Gatsby gets his ideas from books—perhaps because that is how Fitzgerald got his own ideas. Throughout *The Great Gatsby* the passage of time (and the currency or obsolescence of ideas) is marked by texts.

Certain texts themselves enter the text, as in Fitzgerald's retelling of the Horatio Alger plot. Alger is usually perceived as having provided for Fitzgerald and other writers the essential plot of rising from poverty through success in business. But a good deal more seems to have been involved. The Alger stories are full of the kind of resentment about class, style, and wealth that Fitzgerald often expressed in his writing and in the fictions he invented of his own life. Alger applies to Fitzgerald's art and life not only because he tells the great modern story of "rising" to "success" but also because he has such a clear sense of the enemies of promise. Alger is both a guide to the action and a standard of irony. . . .

The characters of *The Great Gatsby* absorb ideas and feelings from what is communicated to them. It might be said that their closest relationships are not with each other—and certainly not with family or community or tradition—but with published, advertised, and perceived images and print. As the narrative begins Nick Carraway tells us how far we are from family, tradition, and clan; on the last page of most editions he states our irretrievable distance from historical beginnings. Much of the narrative in between registers the advent of ideas and values from other kinds of sources.

Carraway as Narrator

Scott Donaldson

"Nick Carraway is a snob," writes Scott Donaldson, editor of *Critical Essays on F. Scott Fitzgerald's* The Great Gatsby. Nick, the narrator, is generally disdainful of the rest of humanity—including Gatsby—and treats the preservation of decorum as a virtue greater than honesty. However, his ability to overcome his personal contempt makes him the perfect narrator for the book, declares Donaldson: His eventual commitment to Gatsby, despite his reluctance and his snobbery, helps persuade the reader to make a similar commitment to understanding the novel's protagonist.

Nick Carraway is a snob. He dislikes people in general and denigrates them in particular. He dodges emotional commitments. Neither his ethical code nor his behavior is exemplary: propriety rather than morality guides him. He is not entirely honest about himself and frequently misunderstands others. Do these shortcomings mean that Nick is an unreliable narrator? At times and in part, yes. But they also mean that he is the perfect narrator for *The Great Gatsby*, and hence it is true that Fitzgerald's greatest technical achievement in the novel was to invent this narrative voice at once "within and without" the action.[1]

The first clue to Nick's makeup comes on the first page of the book, where he totally misunderstands his father's advice. "Whenever you feel like criticizing any one," his father

1. The subject of Nick's character and competence as narrator has been examined at length in many critical articles. Among the most important are Thomas A. Hanzo, "The Theme and the Narrator of *The Great Gatsby*," *Modern Fiction Studies*, 2 (1956–1957), 183–90; Jerome Thale, "The Narrator as Hero," Twentieth Century Literature, 3 (1957), 69–73; R.W. Stallman, "Gatsby and the Hole in Time," *The House that James Built and Other Literary Studies* (East Lansing: Michigan State University Press, 1961), pp. 131–50; Gary J. Scrimgeour, "Against *The Great Gatsby*," *Criticism*, 8 (1966), 75–86; Charles Thomas Samuels, "The Greatness of 'Gatsby,'" *Massachusetts Review*, 7 (1966), 785–94; and Richard Foster, "The Way to Read *Gatsby*," *Sense and Sensibility in Twentieth Century Writing: A Gathering in Memory of William Van O'Connor*, ed. Brom Weber (Carbondale: Southern Illinois University Press, 1970), pp. 94–108.

had told him in his "younger and more vulnerable years," he was to remember that not everyone had enjoyed "the advantages" he has had. Clearly Nick's father is advising tolerance here, and it seems likely that he had detected in his son a propensity to find fault. Nick, however, interprets the remark as a judgment on others, who—lacking what he calls that "sense of the fundamental decencies . . . unequally parcelled out at birth"—consequently misbehave. This interpretation, Nick acknowledges, is an extraordinarily snobbish one, the interpretation of a snob who admits to the charge as if to say that there are far worse things than snobbery in the world: bad manners, for example. Nick's undoubted "advantages," which include good schools, social position, family background, and even an exclusive senior society at Yale, may eventuate in an awareness of the "fundamental decencies" if one construes the phrase narrowly as conforming to conventional standards of propriety, but they hardly guarantee any moral acumen. So it is with Nick Carraway. Most of all he disapproves of those who do *not know how to act.* That is why it takes him so long to ascertain that Jay Gatsby, a walking compendium of social gaucheries, is nonetheless worth any number of Buchanans.

Nick's misunderstanding of his father should also put us on guard against his claim that he's "inclined to reserve all judgments," especially when in the next breath he speaks of the "veteran bores" and "wild, unknown men" who have made him privy to "intimate revelations . . . usually plagiaristic and marred by obvious suppressions." Had they suppressed less, Nick might have been more interested. "Reserving judgments is a matter of infinite hope," he observes, and he is not the character in the novel possessed by infinite hope. He listens to confessions since he is "a little afraid of missing something" otherwise: a vicarious sense of having drunk his cup to the lees. But he does not suspend judgment. In fact, he judges, and condemns, practically everyone he meets in the course of the novel.

Collectively he speaks of closing off his interest in the "abortive sorrows and short-winded elations of men." Introducing individual specimens of this sorry genus, he delineates more specific physical deficiencies. Tom Buchanan has straw hair, a hard mouth, a supercilious manner, and a cruel body with which he pushes people around. There had been men at Yale who hated his guts, and if Nick is not among them, it's not because he can't see why. His wife Daisy, Nick's second cousin once removed, speaks in a thrilling voice, but she murmurs so low that people must bend toward her to hear. Her insincere remark about having "been everywhere and seen everything and done everything" strikes Nick as "a trick of some sort" to exact an emotional commitment from him.

With the lower orders Nick is still less charitable. Myrtle Wilson, smoldering with vitality, carries her "excess flesh sensuously" and comically takes on airs in the West 158th St. apartment Tom has secured for their rendezvous. Meyer Wolfsheim is presented as a small Jew with tiny eyes, a flat nose (in whose nostrils "fine growths of hair" luxuriate), and cuff buttons made of "finest specimens of human molars." Sentence is passed rapidly on minor characters. Myrtle's sister Catherine—"a slender, worldly girl of thirty" with a sticky bob of red hair, rakishly painted eyebrows, and eternally jangling bracelets—is disposed of in a paragraph. And in the catalog of those who attend Gatsby's parties, people are labeled and found wanting by name alone. "The Dancies came, too, and S.B. Whitebait, who was well over sixty, and Maurice A. Flink, and the Hammerheads, and Beluga the tobacco importer, and Beluga's girls": something is fishy here.

Nick's basic contempt for mankind emerges in what he says and thinks as well as in descriptions of others. His particular way of telling the story—his voice—has been variously characterized in the critical literature on *Gatsby,* but surely a dominant characteristic of that voice is its irony.[2] This sometimes leads to light-hearted bantering in conversation, as with Daisy. Is she missed in Chicago, she asks? "All the cars have the left rear wheel painted black as a mourning wreath," he answers, "and there's a persistent wail all night along the north shore."[3] Would Nick like to hear about the butler's nose, she inquires? "That's why I came over to-

---

2. Among those who have called attention to Nick's irony and to his comic sense are Foster and E. Fred Carlisle, "The Triple Vision of Nick Carraway," *Modern Fiction Studies,* 11 (1965–1966), 351–60. On the subject of Nick's multiple voices, see Carlisle; Tom Burnam, "The Eyes of Dr. Eckleburg: A Re-examination of *The Great Gatsby,*" *College English,* 14 (1952), 7–12; A.E. Elmore, "Nick Carraway's Self-Introduction," *Fitzgerald/Hemingway Annual 1971,* ed. Matthew J. Bruccoli and C.E. Frazer Clark (Washington, D.C.: Microcard Editions, 1971), pp. 130–47; and Oliver H. Evans, "'A Sort of Moral Attention': The Narrator of *The Great Gatsby,*" *Fitzgerald/Hemingway Annual 1971,* pp. 117–29.
3. But notice how this casual remark gains resonance from subsequent events related to the motif of careless driving.

night," he responds. His unspoken thoughts, however, tend toward a more "hostile levity": toward sarcasm, in fact.

In his mind Nick constantly puts others down. After listening to Tom Buchanan maunder on about impending racial struggles and the increasing (or is it declining?) heat of the sun, he devastates the man he has helped cuckold when, with his eyes finally opened to the affair between Daisy and Gatsby, Tom begins to expound on the scientific proof for his "second sight" and then stops, the "immediate contingency" having "pulled him back from the edge of the theoretical abyss." Soon after, Nick characterizes Tom's hypocritical defense of family solidarity as "impassioned gibberish." Buchanan probably deserves such treatment, but what of poor Henry Gatz who proudly shows Nick his dead son's schedule for self-improvement, written on the fly-leaf of his copy of *Hopalong Cassidy?* "He was reluctant to close the book, reading each item aloud and then looking eagerly at me. I think he rather expected me to copy down the list for my own use," Nick sniffily observes. Then there is the "persistent undergraduate" who brings Jordan Baker to one of Gatsby's parties under the impression that sooner or later she will "yield him up her person." When that prospect seems unlikely to develop, the undergraduate becomes engaged in "an obstetrical conversation with two chorus girls" and "implore[s]" Nick to join him. As Wolfsheim remarks in another sense, he has "a wrong man." Nick is not interested in making improper connections. He's not interested in making any *lasting* connections at all.

A PATTERN OF EMOTIONAL EVASION

Nick carefully avoids emotional entanglements. He writes letters signed "Love, Nick" to a girl back home, but one reason he's come to New York is to avoid "being rumored into marriage" with her. Unable to stop thinking how "a faint mustache of perspiration" develops on her upper lip when she plays tennis, he severs the relationship. In the East he has "a short affair with a girl who live[s] in Jersey City and work[s] in the accounting department," but lets it "blow quietly away" when her brother begins "throwing mean looks" in his direction.[4] Jordan, his social peer, poses a more seri-

---

4. The word "affair" probably did not carry the specific meaning of sexual liaison in 1925. One of Fitzgerald's friends and contemporaries from St. Paul, Xandra Kalman, uses the word in a far more general sense.

ous threat to his bachelor status. He is attracted to her hard, jaunty body and superior chin-in-air attitude, even though he knows she will lie to avoid responsibility and cheat to win at golf. But in the end she seems too much of a piece with Tom and Daisy, so he breaks off with her, too, before returning to the Middle West. It is not surprising that Nick has reached thirty without being married or engaged: he does not reserve judgment, he reserves himself.[5] Prufrock-like, he contemplates his future: "a decade of loneliness, a thinning list of single men to know, a thinning briefcase of enthusiasm, thinning hair."

In the light of this pattern of evasion, one regards with suspicion Nick's claim that releasing himself from a "vague understanding" with the girl back home before pursuing another with Jordan makes him "one of the few honest people" he's ever known.[6] In fact he regards telling the truth as less important than avoiding the unseemly. A case in point is his remark that Catherine had shown "a surprising amount of character" at Myrtle's inquest by falsely swearing that her sister "had been into no mischief whatever," thus averting a public scandal. Decorum ranks extremely high on his scale of values—certainly higher than honesty.

He demonstrates a similar pattern on the question of sexual morality. References to adultery abound in *The Great Gatsby*. It is rather the expected thing among the idle rich—as Jordan says, Daisy "ought to have something in her life"—and among the "guests" at Gatsby's parties, though only those who contract liaisons with lovers of higher social standing (Myrtle and Gatsby) are punished for their sin or for their presumptuousness. What is Nick's attitude about this extramarital coupling? It depends: what concerns him most is how people *act*, not what they *do*. Daisy, he thinks, should "rush out of the house, child in arms" upon discovering Tom's infidelity. At the same time Nick is not particularly shocked to discover that Tom has "some woman in New York." What he cannot approve of, however, is the way Tom

---

5. Samuels, p. 791, makes the same point.
6. Susan Resneck Parr, "Individual Responsibility in *The Great Gatsby*," *Virginia Quarterly Review* 57 (1981), 662–80, points out that Fitzgerald changed "one of the few decent people" to "one of the few honest people" in revision. Other revisions "added material which stressed Nick's belief in his own honesty and deleted passages which might undercut Nick's integrity," such as his offering the keys of his house to Gatsby and Daisy. In the earliest surviving manuscript, apparently, Fitzgerald had made Nick too obviously untrustworthy a narrator.

conducts the affair. He takes his mistress to popular restaurants to show her off, for example, and then leaves her to
chat with acquaintances. He also concocts the lie that Daisy
is Catholic to explain why he cannot be divorced. As voyeur,
Nick is curious to see Tom's girl; as snob he has no desire to
meet her. When they do meet, she proves a veritable model
of social pretentiousness. In clothes, in gestures, in conversation, she is, simply, ridiculous; not until Tom breaks her
nose does she merit any sympathy whatever.

Nick himself seems almost ridiculous when, in his obsession with propriety, he twice insists on having actually been
invited to Gatsby's first party, unlike most of the gate crash-
ers. Moreover, although all around him people are conducting themselves "according to the rules of behavior associated with amusement parks," he repeatedly tries to meet
and thank his host, as at a formal gathering. This proves difficult, and meanwhile Jordan turns up, relieving him of the
danger of addressing "cordial remarks to passers-by." When
he finally does encounter Gatsby later in the evening, Nick is
caught off guard: he'd been expecting "a florid and corpulent
person in his middle years." For a long time Gatsby continues to confound Nick's expectations. Unlike almost everyone
else in his world, Gatsby resists classification.

A Belief in Gatsby, Not in His Stories

It's not merely that he's curious about Gatsby: *everyone's* curious about Gatsby, this young man who "drift[ed] coolly out
of nowhere and [bought] a palace on Long Island Sound." But
while others merely speculate about his relationship with
von Hindenburg or his career as killer, Nick is exposed
through two rather remarkable coincidences—moving in
next door and knowing Daisy—to more intimate revelations
from the figure of mystery himself. Gatsby's first preposterous account (wealthy parents from the middle west city of
San Francisco, war hero educated at Oxford who subsequently "lived like a young rajah in all the capitals of Europe
. . . collecting jewels, chiefly rubies, hunting big game, painting a little . . . and trying to forget something very sad. . .".)
tends to confirm Nick in his view of his neighbor as preten-
tious arriviste, inventing a background to replace the one he
lacks. Though Gatsby produces the medal from Montenegro
and the cricket photograph, Nick is not persuaded. "Then it
was all true," he proclaims in humorous overstatement. "I

saw the skins of tigers flaming in his palace on the Grand Canal; I saw him opening a chest of rubies to ease, with their crimson-lighted depths, the gnawings of his broken heart." Nick's cynicism on this score is underlined in two subsequent incidents. Stopped for speeding, Gatsby flashes the policeman a white card which purchases instant immunity. "What was that?" Nick asks. "The picture of Oxford?" Later, during the tour of the mansion (and after the lavish display of shirts), Nick has a characteristically sardonic thought: "I was going to ask to see the rubies when the phone rang . . .".

NICK'S POINT OF VIEW

In order to communicate the meaning of *The Great Gatsby*, Fitzgerald had to find a narrator whose presence on the scene is acceptable, who does not find the scene so alien and forbidding that he is incapable of doing it justice, but who is also able (partly because of his separation, but also because of his involvement) to define and describe its meaning and to judge it unobnoxiously. This character is Nick Carraway. We must first of all be sure of his acceptability as a character in this role. He tells us from the start that he is "inclined to reserve all judgments," that he is "slow-thinking and full of interior rules that act as brakes on [his] desires"; but he also admits to great admiration for the kind of "extraordinary gift for hope, a romantic readiness," which he sees in Gatsby. Carraway's background is sketched in sufficiently to enable us to see the sources of his point of view. It is Midwestern, traditional, contained; most important is its stability, which comes from his family's having lived in the same place, even the same house, for several generations. Extreme mobility, in both Gatsby's and Buchanan's case, is a moral liability.

Frederick J. Hoffman, *The Great Gatsby: A Study*, 1962.

Under the circumstances Nick hardly expects *any* section of Gatsby's fabulous story to be true, and when Gatsby modifies his tale to explain why and for how long he'd actually gone to Oxford, Nick is willing to put all the young rajah balderdash out of mind: "I had one of those renewals of complete faith in him that I'd experienced before." Clearly, one part of Nick wants to believe in Gatsby, just as another part holds him up for ridicule.

The snob in Nick Carraway finds Gatsby contemptible. He makes the point both on page two [in the Scribner Library

Edition] of the novel ("Gatsby . . . represented everything for which I have an unaffected scorn") and on page one hundred fifty-four (". . . I disapproved of him from beginning to end"). Significantly, this second statement immediately follows Nick's "You're worth the whole damn bunch put together" speech. He can simultaneously praise Gatsby, in other words, and still disapprove of the "gorgeous pink rag of a suit" he's wearing, scorn his "old sport" affectation, disapprove of his ostentatious Hotel de Ville and extravagant parties; scorn his shady business "gonnegtions"—above all, disapprove of Gatsby's social incompetence.

Gatsby obviously lacks that "sense of the fundamental decencies" that comes with the right background. He seems to think that his awful parties are socially respectable gatherings. He does not take in the situation when Tom Buchanan, Mr. Sloane, and "the lady" with Mr. Sloane stop by and the lady invites him and Nick to dinner. As Nick sees at once, no matter what the lady said, "Mr. Sloane had determined" that Gatsby shouldn't come along. By declining the invitation himself, Nick provides his neighbor with a model to emulate. But Gatsby ignores the clue, and so is humiliated when, as he changes clothes to accompany the others, they ride off without him. The following Saturday night, at Gatsby's next party, Nick is startled to witness his socially inept host dancing a "graceful, conservative fox-trot." Yet this is the man whose affair with Daisy he facilitates by inviting the two of them for tea ("Don't bring Tom," he warns her) and whose continuing relationship he encourages by "remaining watchfully in the garden" while they talk on the steps of his house for half an hour. The question is why. For one thing, Jordan asked him to arrange the tea; for another, Nick dislikes Tom and knows of his unfaithfulness and brutality. Yet he would not have so willingly played the role of go-between had he not felt a curious kinship with the "elegant young roughneck" in the mansion next door.

A Pair of Romantics

The fact is that both Nick and Gatsby have romantic inclinations. The difference is that Gatsby guides his life by his dream, while Nick carefully separates romance from reality. What he most admires in Gatsby is the "extraordinary gift for hope," the "romantic readiness" he has found in no one else. . . .

Nick imagines glamorous encounters, but reads about banking after dinner in the Yale Club. Gatsby makes his fortune, and sets out to capture the rest of his dream. Because of his remarkable commitment to that dream—exactly the sort of commitment Nick declines to make—Nick can almost forgive Gatsby his presumption in courting Daisy under cover of a uniform that let "her believe he was a person from much the same stratum as herself . . .". Because of it he can very nearly pardon Gatsby's taking Daisy "one still October night," taking her "because he had no real right to touch her hand." Because of it, too, he can temporarily efface from memory Gatsby's tactless offer of a chance to "pick up a nice bit of money" in return for arranging the meeting with Daisy. On the evidence it's clear that Gatsby as parvenu will manage to do or say the wrong thing if given an opportunity to do so. Yet Nick finally puts aside his offended sense of propriety and decides to stick it out with Gatsby. After his death, in fact, "it grew upon me [Nick] that I was responsible, because no one else was interested—interested, I mean, with that intense personal interest to which every one has some vague right at the end." In the end, and for the only time in his life, Nick makes a commitment himself. And it is because this decision is so difficult for him, a judgmental snob who invariably keeps his emotional distance, that it seems inevitable for the rest of us. That is why he is the right narrator for *The Great Gatsby.*

Carraway and Fitzgerald Share Moral Immaturity

W.M. Frohock

Fitzgerald deserves praise for inventing the character of Nick Carraway, the narrator who has his own, separate life to live during the novel's story, admits W.M. Frohock, who teaches American literature at the University of Lille in France. But Nick is too sentimental and immature to provide a strong moral center for the novel: Although he does not approve of Gatsby, he fails to condemn him as a ruthless crook. The immaturity of Nick's vision, Frohock claims, "is probably indistinguishable from Fitzgerald's."

The issue of style is central in the structure of *The Great Gatsby* because it creates the voice of the "central moral consciousness." In other words, it is the principal means of characterizing Nick Carraway. Fitzgerald has been justly praised for the invention of the Carraway character. The strategy of telling the story through the awareness of a man who has his own independent life going on all the while—his job to do, his off-stage love affair to terminate, his private concerns at West Egg—greatly intensifies what Henry James would have called the "felt life" of the story. As his connection with the main action grows closer, more or less despite his own preferences, the novel develops a dimension of density as palpable as what Joseph Conrad achieves in the stories which are told through the character of Marlowe, combined with a kind of naturalness Conrad hardly tried to manage. To have brought him off so well is enough to put Fitzgerald in that small category of novelists who really know what they are doing. But there still remains the question whether Nick Carraway is the central moral consciousness this novel needed to satisfy the rather stringent de-

From *Strangers to This Ground: Cultural Diversity in Contemporary American Writing* by W.M. Frohock (Dallas: Southern Methodist University Press, 1961). Reprinted by permission of the Estate of W.M. Frohock.

mands of a criticism which requires, in addition to structural perfection, real depth of moral perception.

UNABLE TO THINK AND FEEL AT THE SAME TIME

Nick is not supposed to be a fool. He has had what his father calls "the advantages": an attentive bringing-up and a Yale education. War and peace have given him opportunity to observe people under stress. He has at least normal social experience and social acumen. At thirty he is quite representative of the kind of American who has had most of the privileges his country has to offer. Moreover, his heart is in the right place; his emotions are warm and easily stirred; he is capable of separating his loyalties from his peculiar personal interests. But it must be added that he has more compassion than brains. He is unable to feel and think, at the same time, about the matter at hand.

His feelings eventually tell him that something is very wrong and put him very firmly on the side of Gatsby, this man of whom, he makes it very clear, he does not "approve." He does not believe the story Gatsby tells about the war and Oxford, but as he listens his "incredulity" becomes submerged in "fascination." He knows perfectly well that Gatsby's secretiveness about his business is shady, but even after he meets Meyer Wolfsheim, the man who bought the Black Sox, he never quite gets it through his head that Gatsby is not only a successful but also a cheap crook. Just as he realizes with no great effort that Jordan Baker is "incurably dishonest" without the facts "making any difference" to him—he is just "casually sorry"—he lets Gatsby's crookedness make no difference to him by seeing it, through a curtain of sentimentality, as an instrument for attaining what Nick regularly calls "the Dream."

So far as Nick is concerned, we never find out just exactly what the Dream is. Every time the subject comes up, he slides off into gooey sentiment. . . .

But the more inkling one gets of what the Dream consists of, the more clearly one sees that surely it is nothing very pretty. James Gatz, the farm boy from Minnesota, gets the notion he can have all the gratifications he wants if only he will work hard enough. These gratifications come to sum themselves up in the person of Daisy, who eventually marries Tom Buchanan. Gatsby retains her, even so, as an emblem of his acquisitive drive. But this drive, we remember, was formed before he ever saw Daisy. "So he invented," Nick tells us, "just the sort of Jay Gatsby a seventeen-year-old boy would be likely to invent, and to this conception he was faithful to the end." This comes down to saying, simply, that Gatsby's career was the result of putting the lethal powers of a ruthless man at the service of an adolescent wish-fulfillment. He emerges as a case of arrested development, of juvenile delinquency physically grown up.

THE INVENTION OF NICK

Nearly every critic of *The Great Gatsby* has stressed the tremendous structural importance of the narrator, Nick Carraway, the character through whom Fitzgerald is able to achieve that aesthetic distance from his own experience necessary for firmness of control and clarity of perception, through whom he can express that delicately poised ambiguity of moral vision, the sense of being "within and without, simultaneously enchanted and repelled by the inexhaustible variety of life" out of which insight into the truth of things must grow. William Troy has summed it up neatly and concisely:

> In the earlier books author and hero tended to melt into one another because there was no internal principle of differentiation by which they might be separated; they respired in the same climate, emotional and moral; they were tarred with the same brush. But in *Gatsby* is achieved a dissociation, by which Fitzgerald was able to isolate one part of himself, the spectatorial or esthetic, and also the more intelligent and responsible, in the person of the ordinary but quite sensible narrator, from another part of himself, the dream-ridden romantic adolescent from St. Paul and Princeton, in the person of the legendary Jay Gatsby.

W.J. Harvey, *English Studies*, February 1957.

But the power of Gatsby's dream blinds Nick to the obvious and his sense of fair play also confuses issues. From people like Tom and Daisy Gatsby has had a bad deal. "'They're a rotten crowd,' I shouted across the lawn. 'You're worth the whole damn bunch put together.'" He adds in the next paragraph that this was the only compliment he ever gave Gatsby, because he "disapproved of him from beginning to end." Possibly the compliment should not be considered a very great one, since it compared Gatsby with people of no high moral quality; but Nick has just said, also, that Gatsby was following some sort of Grail, which is a strong enough expression in the circumstances to make it clear that Nick is not aware of his own moral ambivalence.

Nick's sincerity is unexceptionable. He is deeply disturbed by Gatsby's disaster; it becomes his own. Gatsby's death ends a chapter in his own life: he gives up his house, sells his car to the grocer, quits his job, sees Tom and Jordan one last time, and then takes his "provincial squeamishness" back to his home in the Middle West—thus tacking something typically American on a novel which, in general pattern, belongs to the category whose prototype is Honoré de Balzac's *Lost Illusions.* His dream, as well as Gatsby's, has been shattered—and he finally identifies himself with the myriad young men who have left the shelter of home to discover that life is not so enchanting as they have been brought up to expect. What makes this particular version of a familiar theme so specifically American is his laying blame on his having passed from one cultural area to another. Fitzgerald's reader will agree that something in Nick's development has prevented his reaching the moral maturity which would have allowed him to perceive Gatsby's "appalling sentimentality" without falling away into sentimentality himself—as we have seen him do in this prose, which is not only Fitzgerald's style but also Nick's characterizing utterance.

In the famous article on Gustave Flaubert, Henry James deplores that the master should have placed in the center of *Madame Bovary* and *The Sentimental Education* such "mean" moral consciences as Emma Bovary and Frédéric Moreau. To call Nick Carraway "mean" would be manifestly unfair, but there would be nothing unfair in calling him inadequate for the job. At thirty he is still too young for the moral responsibility it involves.

IMMATURE CHARACTERS
REFLECT THE AUTHOR'S INEXPERIENCE

A final estimate of Fitzgerald has to include the fact of his preferring such immature characters for the point of view. Rosemary turns eighteen in *Tender Is the Night*; [in *The Last Tycoon*] Cecilia is no more than twenty and still an undergraduate at Bennington. At thirty, Nick shares their disadvantage. What each of them is busy trying to pick through is not the surface of an ethically complex situation but the eggshell of his own emotional and social inexperience. The distance which separates such instruments of the moral imagination from one on the order of Lambert Strether [in Henry James's *The Ambassadors*] is vertiginous.

All this suggests that Fitzgerald falls somewhat short of the eminence as moralist which recent criticism would like to attribute to him. Actually, there is some reason to doubt that Fitzgerald was really devoted to the use of the central moral consciousness as such; i.e., he used it, but not especially for the purposes of the moralist. From his notes and scenarios for *The Last Tycoon* it is clear that he meant originally to have Cecilia narrate the action and thus rigidly restrict the point of view, but it is also clear from the finished parts of the book that this strategy did not appeal to him strongly enough to cause him to rebuild his story in a way that would make its use plausible. Similarly, Rosemary serves as point of view character in only a relatively small section of *Tender Is the Night,* after which she becomes merely another member of the novel's population. One has to conclude that if the temporarily central position of these characters was important to Fitzgerald, the reason for the importance has no connection with moral observation. For such a character to be a useful means of indirect moral analysis he would have, obviously, to maintain his privileged position throughout the story, the end of which should be at least as morally significant as the beginning.

Dealing with Manners, not Morals

Nick's inability to break through the murk and see Gatsby for what he really is—a pitiable romantic oaf—and his missing the fundamental preposterousness of the yarn about the poor boy who beat his way to fortune for love of the girl who spurned him, and then got killed for his pains, is probably indistinguishable from Fitzgerald's. It does not seem to have perturbed many among his audience, and I suspect the reason is that most of his audience do not take Fitzgerald to be a moralist at all. They take Gatsby's career as being all of a piece with the sensibility which did not object to ending a paragraph with a cliché about life's inexhaustible variety.

For its proper purpose, that sensibility is a perfectly useful one. But the purpose has to do not with morals but with manners. It was because Fitzgerald was dealing essentially with manners that he could work so hard on the "central" characters of two of his novels, only to let them drop back out of their central positions. Their role was to introduce the reader to, and ease him into, a new strange world; once he was acclimated their importance declined. They were there to help him report the "feel" of a certain kind of life, the precise sensation of it. And because, after all, "felt life" is a synonym for "novel," we honor Fitzgerald's achievement.

Images of Death

James E. Miller Jr.

A vast ash heap, beneath Dr. T.J. Eckleburg's staring oculist billboard, spreads a pall of death over *The Great Gatsby*, notes author and American literature critic James E. Miller Jr. Images of death proliferate throughout the novel.

The Great Gatsby progresses by images. At the opening of Chapter II, Fitzgerald reveals what might be called the controlling image of the book, the first of a series of subtly interrelated images of death in life, life in death:

> About half way between West Egg and New York the motor road hastily joins the railroad and runs beside it for a quarter of a mile, so as to shrink away from a certain desolate area of land. This is a valley of ashes—a fantastic farm where ashes grow like wheat into ridges and hills and grotesque gardens; where ashes take the forms of houses and chimneys and rising smoke and, finally, with a transcendent effort, of men who move dimly and already crumbling through the powdery air. Occasionally a line of gray cars crawls along an invisible track, gives out a ghastly creak, and comes to rest, and immediately the ash-gray men swarm up with leaden spades and stir up an impenetrable cloud, which screens their obscure operations from your sight.

The reader may hear himself murmur, as he reads, "I had not thought death had undone so many." Fitzgerald's waste land scene is clearly a scene of a living hell, an assemblage of "grotesque gardens" that parody in ashes the vital world of growing things; and it is peopled by living dead men who crumble away even as they rehearse their pointless activities, swallowed finally from view by the clouds of ash-dust raised by their meaningless movement. Over this bizarre scene stare the gigantic eyes of Dr. T.J. Eckleburg, the fading sign of a long-forgotten oculist. Those weather-dimmed eyes, as they "brood on over the solemn dumping ground," will reappear in the novel, coming to haunt it and the

From "Fitzgerald's *Gatsby*: The World as Ash Heap" by James E. Miller Jr., in *The Twenties: Fiction, Poetry, Drama*, edited by Warren French (DeLand, FL: Everett/Edwards, 1975). Reprinted by permission of the author.

reader: the world as ash heap, presided over by the vacant stare of a billboard deity.

IMAGES OF DEATH

Though confined geographically to the area near the Wilson garage, the valley of ashes spreads like a contagious fungus psychically through all the novel, leaving in its wake a trail of images of death. They appear sometimes only on the periphery of vision, as on the drive to New York (Nick with Gatsby): "A dead man passed us in a hearse heaped with blooms, followed by two carriages with drawn blinds, and by more cheerful carriages for friends. The friends looked out at us with the tragic eyes and short upper lips of southeastern Europe, and I was glad that the sight of Gatsby's splendid car was included in their somber holiday." The hearse and its contents may serve as an omen for Gatsby's car, which in spite of its ministering so spectacularly to all the comforts of life (". . . bright with nickel, swollen here and there in its monstrous length with triumphant hat-boxes and supper-boxes and tool-boxes . . . terraced with a labyrinth of wind-shields that mirrored a dozen suns") becomes the novel's chief vehicle of death, leading directly to Myrtle's. Her death, within easy view of the valley of ashes, is as grotesque and meaningless as her life, ripping asunder the body that was the repository of her cheap successes and minor ambitions: ". . .when they had torn open her shirt-waist, still damp with perspiration, they saw her left breast was swinging loose like a flap, and there was no need to listen for the heart beneath. The mouth was wide open and ripped at the corners, as though she had choked a little in giving up the tremendous vitality she had stored so long."

Gatsby's gorgeous cream-colored car is also the indirect cause of his own death, as it is the deep imprint of the fantastic car on his excited brain that enables Wilson (through Tom Buchanan) to track Gatsby down and to shoot him (erroneously, of course) for killing Myrtle. At this critical moment, Gatsby has gone to his pool for a swim, and Nick speculates that for Gatsby it might well have been a moment of awareness—awareness that he had lost Daisy to Tom, and that he had lived "too long with a single dream." As Nick imaginatively recreates the scene, Gatsby is touched with terror at the discovery that the world is not a garden of delights but something of an ash-heap: "He must have looked up at an unfamiliar sky through frightening leaves and shivered as he found what a grotesque thing a rose is and how raw the sunlight was upon the scarcely created grass. A new world, material without being real, where poor ghosts, breathing dreams like air, drifted fortuitously about . . . like that ashen fantastic figure gliding toward him through the amorphous trees." *Ashen.* By now the signal is unmistakable. Though driven by a dream of splendid life, Gatsby plays out his role (like the others) on the dumping ground of ashes. But in contrast with the violence of Myrtle's death, Gatsby's seems hardly noticeable as his body floats silently on the swimming pool surface:

> There was a faint, barely perceptible movement of the water as the fresh flow from one end urged its way toward the drain at the other. With little ripples that were hardly the shadows of waves, the laden mattress moved irregularly down the pool. A small gust of wind that scarcely corrugated the surface was enough to disturb its accidental course with its accidental burden. The touch of a cluster of leaves revolved it slowly, tracing, like the leg of transit, a thin circle in the water.

It is surely the vacuous eyes of Dr. T. J. Eckleburg with their uncomprehending and meaningless stare that preside over this scene of the pneumatic mattress floating aimlessly on "its *accidental* course with its *accidental* burden." In a world become ash-heap, one's fate has no relevance to one's life: *accident* rules supreme.

As the valley of ashes is introduced early in the novel to become a kind of pervasive presence, gradually becoming the psychic setting for all the novel's action, so "the night scene by El Greco" in the last chapter tends to take over the reader's memory of the novel and to distort the action into a kind of surrealist dream. In trying to sum up, finally, his inexplicable feelings about the East, Nick reports the way it appears in his "more fantastic dreams": "I see it as a night scene by El Greco: a hundred houses, at once conventional and grotesque, crouching under a sullen, overhanging sky and a lustreless moon. In the foreground four solemn men in dress suits are walking along the sidewalk with a stretcher on which lies a drunken woman in a white evening dress. Her hand, which dangles over the side, sparkles cold with jewels. Gravely the men turn in at a house—the wrong house. But no one knows the woman's name, and no one cares." The "day scene" of *The Great Gatsby* is surely the valley of ashes, and

its night scene is this El Greco dreamscape, with its meticu-
lously dressed characters performing meaningless actions in
a meaningless world. But there is, perhaps, more connection
between these two powerful images than is explicitly stated.
The night scene by El Greco seems to be the dark underside
of the valley of ashes, the night of its day, the nightmare of its
reality. The one posits the other. And there seems to be a con-
tinuity in the gigantic, vacant oculist's eyes of the valley of
ashes and the "sullen, overhanging sky and . . . lustreless
moon" of the El Greco night scene. The worlds merge and
meld into each other. And in that world, if one looks over his
shoulder, he might well notice a scene out of T.S. Eliot's *The
Waste Land*, Part V:

> A woman drew her long black hair out tight
> And fiddled whisper music on those strings
> And bats and baby faces in the violet light
> Whistled, and beat their wings
> And crawled head downward down a blackened wall.

An Adolescent Version of the American Dream

Michael Vincent Miller

Psychotherapist and author Michael Vincent Miller views *Gatsby* as an illustration of the shortcomings of a romantic culture. Jay Gatsby's beliefs that anything is possible if he wants it enough and that lost love (and every other failure) always gets a second chance are characteristic of a culture arrested at adolescence, Miller cautions.

In my judgment, our finest, most exemplary American parable of romantic tragic failure is F. Scott Fitzgerald's magnificent novel *The Great Gatsby*. It reaches out to explore the possibilities of passionate love in the first half of the twentieth century, the era of burgeoning erotic hedonism, as fully as Nathaniel Hawthorne's *The Scarlet Letter* did the residual sexual puritanism of the nineteenth century. In both novels, a solitary larger-than-life figure loves heroically and thus rises above the mediocrity of his or her surrounding social milieu. There's also an important difference between them: Hester Prynne's compassion and capacity for forgiveness, both toward herself and, more profoundly, toward her far weaker companion in adultery, Arthur Dimmesdale, become a mode of redemption. There is no redemption for Jay Gatsby, a more limited creature spiritually, although a man of great decency and splendid will, who is brought down by his total immersion in the ideals of his time.

Partly, of course, the difference stems from the closing down of redemption in the modern world. The idea of sin, a religious conception of failure, contained within it the idea of a higher forgiveness. But a large enough mistake in judgment in our day can turn out to be, as it was for Gatsby, simply a fatal error. Gatsby's demise hovers between the tragic and the pathetic; there is something almost blind, almost as

From *Intimate Terrorism: The Deterioration of Erotic Life* by Michael Vincent Miller. Copyright © 1995 by Michael Vincent Miller. Reprinted by permission of W.W. Norton & Company, Inc.

random as natural disaster, about the sheer moral stupidity of the surrounding characters' actions, which finally succeed in crushing Gatsby to death.

DEMONSTRATING THE FAILURE OF THE AMERICAN DREAM

What makes *The Great Gatsby* so powerful and so important a map of its contemporary social landscape is the lyrical precision with which Fitzgerald, through his narrator Nick Carraway, a perpetual bystander who rarely loses his patience with the ambiguities of individual life, lays open layer upon layer of the American dream and, without sacrificing what is beautiful in it, demonstrates its inevitable, disastrous failure. Its beauty, though, is the beauty of adolescence, enchanting to behold, poetic and meretricious at the same time in how far it will go, in what sublime, almost insane risks it will endure, to realize its stubborn belief that pure wanting can make the fantastic happen. The daring in this youthful journey is awesome, but the product at its end can be so thin—much too thin to cover the blunders of conflicted, imperfect adults as they try to get by and love one another. No other piece of writing about our culture has penetrated as deep, or with such a mixture of sympathy and distaste, into the pulsating interior organs of this dream.

At the end, even Nick turns away in disgust and hopelessness, appalled at what he has seen, what he has been called upon, despite himself, to participate in. For the American dream, as Fitzgerald conceives it, is ultimately the romantic dream of becoming whoever you want to be, of good fortune, if you crave it hard enough, of unlimited, renewable promises, of vast loves inextricable from vast material successes. The allure of romantic culture is a hypnotic beckoning light on the remote horizon or across the dark bay, but when you get too close in broad daylight and try to make it too real, Fitzgerald tells us, much of it turns out to be just tinsel, a cheap glitter.

There are various facets to the glowing image that drives Jay Gatsby to the verge of a seemingly impossible success, only to have it shatter into failure at the last minute. In the first place, there is the combination of discipline, charm, and just plain good luck with which Jay Gatsby, née James Gatz, a poor immigrant farmboy from North Dakota, is able to take himself by the bootstraps and revise himself, fitting himself into a role that he has for so long envied and fantasized about. Opportunity knocks at the door of those who are prepared to make full use of it—this is the premise by which he conducts his life. We learn only after his death and in the most touching way how early in his life Gatsby's fierce resolve to get ahead had swelled in his breast, when Henry Gatz, his father, shows Nick a copy of *Hopalong Cassidy* with his son's spartan schedule and list of good intentions hand-printed on the rear flyleaf. It's the new liberalized Puritan ethic, in which living by austere rules and good works *does* earn you a place among the elect right here and now on earth; one no longer has to pray for rewards in the next life, which are contingent upon the unfathomable will of God.

Of course, in our secular version, we have replaced God with the venture capitalist, a wealthy investor willing to place his faith in someone with empty pockets but a brilliant, marketable idea. And indeed, Gatsby finds his venture capitalists, even though his only brilliant idea is his self-made personality, a gorgeous "unbroken series of successful gestures" and a "heightened sensitivity to the promises of life, . . . an extraordinary gift for hope, a romantic readiness." First, a millionaire from the Far West named Dan Cody discovers him at seventeen, takes him aboard his yacht as his right-hand man, and sails off to distant ports, showing Gatsby the wonders open to the very rich. When Cody dies a few years later, Gatsby is penniless again, but now his fantasies are fleshed out with palpable experience. After serving in the army, he is forced to turn to the gambler Meyer Wolfsheim, who found him hungry and broke in a poolroom and picked him up on the basis of his charm. Wolfsheim enables Gatsby to become fabulously wealthy through making him a partner in shady deals—bootlegging, illegal maneuvers in the financial markets, and other criminal ventures.

In one sense, all this adds up to nothing more than a darker and more colossal version of the bourgeois hope that one will accumulate enough to own a bigger house, buy a flashy car, and have a great social life. In portraying Gatsby's royal mansion on Long Island Sound, his dazzling yellow Rolls-Royce convertible, his bureau drawers spilling over with expensive shirts, and his outrageously generous parties, Fitzgerald has inflated this part of the dream to a grandiosity of baroque proportions. Whatever shabby means it takes to get there, at moments the glories of material opu-

lence turn into pure song. As Nick describes the settings of
Gatsby's lavish parties,

> There was music from my neighbor's house through the
> summer nights. In his blue gardens men and girls came and
> went like moths among the whisperings and the champagne
> and the stars. . . . On weekends his Rolls-Royce became an
> omnibus, bearing parties to and from the city. . . . Every Fri-
> day five crates of oranges and lemons arrived from a fruiter
> in New York. . . . On buffet tables, garnished with glistening
> hors-d'oeuvre, spiced baked hams crowded against salads of
> harlequin designs and pastry pigs and turkeys bewitched to
> a dark gold.

COURTSHIP AS CONSPICUOUS CONSUMPTION

But to Gatsby, these riches have become by now almost in-
cidentals; they are the means—as if courtship were a matter
of conspicuous consumption—by which to impress and win
the great romantic love of his life, the belle from Louisville,
Daisy Buchanan. This is the final, almost religious meaning
of Gatsby's quest. In the most refined versions of medieval
courtly love, passionate commitment to the idealized other,
resulting in the performance of sacred duties and services
on her behalf, built the stairway for a spiritual ascent. *The
Great Gatsby* borrows some of this and converts it into an
epic poem of American upward mobility wedded to romantic love. It doesn't matter that for a flash in the gray aftertaste
of the next morning, it all looks suspiciously like little more
than a teenage boy, in the heat of his first infatuation with
the most popular girl at school, who drives by her house in
his new car hoping to capture her interest.

Theodore Dreiser's *An American Tragedy*, published in
1925, the same year as *The Great Gatsby*, diagrams much of
the same territory, although Dreiser views the relations between love and material success with a much more
cold-blooded eye than Fitzgerald. The Darwinian bare bones
stick out in *An American Tragedy*, since there is hardly
enough romantic coverlet to disguise the hero's naked ambition, and he cynically exploits his two girls—the first for
sex and a bit of solace for the lonely life that goes with working in a factory; the second, a rich man's daughter, whom he
intends to marry mainly as the vehicle for finally achieving
status and power. Most significantly, the emphases in these
two novels are practically the inverse of one another:
Whereas romance is only the means to wealth in Dreiser's

tale, wealth becomes both means and end, inseparable from romantic fulfillment, in Fitzgerald's. Both novels show us that the holy quest for success, driven by whatever force of impulse, must come to grief—the more driven, it seems, the more dramatic the final failure. Both Gatsby and Dreiser's hero, Clyde Griffiths, aspire with terrific will. But because his idealism transfigures the crass materials provided by his culture and because he is fundamentally decent and sensitive to others, we mourn Gatsby's pointless, misguided execution more deeply than that of Griffiths, whose punishment comes much closer than Gatsby's to being what he deserved.

TRYING TO RETRIEVE A LOST LOVE

The other central theme of romantic adolescence in *The Great Gatsby* is that you can always go back and retrieve what appears to be irretrievably lost. Gatsby has dedicated his entire life to an idyllic month five years earlier when he and Daisy met and fell in love just before the army sent him overseas. That month for him is frozen in time forever. When Nick tells him that you can't repeat the past, Gatsby answers, "Why of course you can!" Gatsby's faith is the consummation of romantic culture's unshakable belief in the second chance at a great love that has been lost: Clinging to it is supposed to lead the way back through the gates of paradise, a journey that will end in the very arms of the idealized lost beloved.

Vacillating between her marriage to an abusive, unfaithful husband and the lure of Gatsby's ferocious love, Daisy Buchanan is simply no match for the myth that Gatsby has constructed. When he insists that she return his perfect loyalty to their original meeting, she replies, "Oh you want too much." From that instant forward it's clear that Gatsby is doomed. Daisy has moved on, not to something more wholesome or mature, but to a confused and torn resignation from which she spends her time distracting herself. She has given herself up to a dependence on the secure power and wealth of old money, thus conforming to the upper-crust values she was born to, and she is not about to risk it now for the suspicious new wealth of Gatsby, even though her security takes the form of Tom Buchanan, her brutally dominating husband. Daisy is not being inconsistent at all: In love with Jay Gatsby five years ago, and probably still in love with him, she is simply repeating what she did last time, when, no longer able to wait for Gatsby's return from the army, and not wishing to go against her parents' and her society's expectations, she married Buchanan in the first place.

The Great Gatsby, for all its wonders, offers us little besides two alternatives for intimacy and marriage, two polar extremes by which to measure how to love, both unsatisfactory, both destined to failure. Take your choice: either Gatsby's impossible, illusory adolescent ideal of romantic perfection, or the callous disregard for others and resignation toward one another that characterize the self-centered Buchanans, who are far worse than Willa Cather's Henshawes [in *My Mortal Enemy*] in that they are beyond either illusion or disillusionment. Our hearts go out to the poetic, self-created Gatsby, but how can we believe in him or make use of his almost fanatical adherence to an impossible dream?

The failure of virtually everyone in *The Great Gatsby* is not merely human nature; it's largely due to the blight—and Gatsby himself is by no means uncontaminated by it—that they have absorbed from their culture, that strange fusion of greed and idealism, power and sexual love, that too often exemplifies America's greatest aspirations as much as its lowest. Fitzgerald's dissection of it displays the sickness at its heart. In a way, Jay Gatsby is an American descendant of Gustave Flaubert's Emma Bovary. He is just as filled as she with yearnings to break through the restrictions of his background, the gray destiny his social class would have afforded him, just as intent on acquiring the freedom and power that wealth, status, and romance combined seem to provide for self-fulfillment. If he bears a family likeness to Emma Bovary, however, it is Emma crossed with Captain Ahab—a Darwinian, inevitably male version of Emma, an Emma who grew up in the vast empty spaces of North Dakota and who brought the myth of the frontier to Long Island Sound.

Both *Madame Bovary* and *The Great Gatsby* present us with fascinating characters who refuse to settle for the given limits of the social or even the human condition. Both Emma and Gatsby feed in adolescence on popular images of romance to inflate their hopes. And both use this imagery to create new selves, as though the self is all surface and appearance—the manners, expensive clothes, and paraphernalia that their cultures treat as the stuff of being desirable. But think of the difference between the dreams of a lonely, poor immigrant boy growing up in the empty spaces of

North Dakota, inheriting the myth of the frontier, and those of a beautiful young woman raised among the petty bourgeoisie in a cramped and busy French rural town. Flaubert's *Madame Bovary* is also about the aspiration to status and wealth through fantasies of romantic love, but it takes place in a society thickly textured with social class and thus with less of the underground raw Darwinian power struggle.

TRYING TO MAKE UP FOR EMOTIONAL SCARCITY

The fixation on eternal youth, the belief that there is always another chance, the feeling that time doesn't really pass, so that life is conceived as boundless opportunity, the struggle to make love last forever—these are the major themes of the culture of romance, a culture arrested at adolescence. It's a potent but unreal myth of infinite abundance, perhaps our most fervent try to make up for underlying emotional scarcity. But it has brought us to an unfortunate pass: Most of us marry out of enthusiasm, which in a way is one of our most heroic gestures. But we travel too lightly for so momentous an expedition. Carrying enough psychological equipment for intimacy only to the point of adolescence, we stop there, and the values of our popular culture help us stay there. After the enthusiasm begins to wane, there is not much left over to deal with the laborious part of it—differences that are hard to reconcile, mistakes and other letdowns, old anxieties that have to be absorbed and metabolized into something useful instead of destructive. Having started on the top of the mountain, we are suddenly deposited once again at the bottom and can't find the inner momentum or external help to work our way back up.

A *Gatsby* for Today

Sven Birkerts

Although *The Great Gatsby* is considered an American classic, Sven Birkerts, author of *American Energies: Essays on Fictions,* claims that it is as relevant to today's world as it is to the world of the 1920s. Because of the excesses of the 1980s, Birkerts writes, America faces the same situation Nick faces: the morning-after hangover. The lesson of the novel is not to avoid the intoxication, Birkerts says, but to learn to alter the outcome—to retain the intoxication's power while accommodating its dreams to reality.

Since it was first published, in 1925, *The Great Gatsby* has established itself as an American classic—more tellingly, as a classic that people actually read, and love. There are some good reasons for this. Fitzgerald's novel is at once formally elegant and piercingly romantic in its expression—a compelling story, but one imbued with the features of legend. It goes off like a flashbulb, freezing a bold array of images on the retina; the fade is delicious, stirring. And then there is the beauty of the writing, the lyric thrill of the sentences. Here is Nick Carraway arriving for his first visit at the home of Daisy and Tom Buchanan:

> Their house was even more elaborate than I expected, a cheerful red-and-white Georgian Colonial mansion, overlooking the bay. The lawn started at the beach and ran toward the front door for a quarter of a mile, jumping over sun-dials and brick walls and burning gardens—finally when it reached the house drifting up the side in bright vines as though from the momentum of its run. The front was broken by a line of French windows, glowing now with reflected gold and wide open to the warm windy evening, and Tom Buchanan in riding clothes was standing with his legs apart on the front porch.

Kinetic and sportive at first, the description comes to rest in a stationary—heraldic—image of power. This is a prose that has learned a few tricks from the movie camera.

From "A Gatsby for Today" by Sven Birkerts, *Atlantic Monthly*, March 1993; © 1993 by Sven Birkerts, as first published in the *Atlantic Monthly*.

But economy and stylistic grace, even when coupled with a good page-turning story, are not enough to ensure that a work will rise above seasonal excellence to become a classic. To attain that status a novel—or a work in any genre—must perpetually renew its relevance for audiences. Some books must wait for changing cultural circumstances to give them point; they go in and out of print as the incalculable mood of the general readership dictates. Others, the true classics, survive the vagaries of the marketplace by tapping the stratum of the universal, embodying our essential dreams and conflicts.

Gatsby succeeds on these latter terms. If the novel is not universal in the Shakespearean or Dantean sense, it is nevertheless thoroughly and perfectly American, a pure distillation of our collective experience. But even as it endures as a classic, *Gatsby* is also able to manifest a particular immediacy at certain times. Just now, I would say, it has a special resonance. Indeed, it might well be a kind of breviary for the nineties, not only because it gives us portraits of our recent and current psychological climates, but also because it tells us something about who we are at a point when we very badly need to know.

There is, of course, the obvious relevance—*Gatsby* as a cautionary tale. The Jazz Age of Fitzgerald's 1920s corresponds in so many ways to our recent 1980s: the glitter and public strut of money, and the fiscal and moral leveraging that made it possible; the reckless rush away from the centers of gravity, and the sudden, terrible realization that gravity writes no exceptions—all this is in the book. The wild party and the hangover. We know it well: morning after in America. Like Nick at the outset of the story, we are waking up, slightly stunned, wondering what happened and what it means. Nick says, "When I came back from the East last autumn I felt that I wanted the world to be in uniform and at a sort of moral attention forever; I wanted no more riotous excursions with privileged glimpses into the human heart."

THE LOGIC OF A DREAM

Gatsby unfolds over the course of a long summer and follows the logic of a dream. One of the marvels of the book is the way in which the narration changes. Though Nick has alerted us in the first few pages to the crashing outcome, we forget. We forget because Nick forgets. His narration becomes fresh and expectant, untainted by hindsight. He is a young man gone east to make his way; he has rented a bungalow next to a fabulous manor house tenanted by a singularly mysterious character.

We first catch sight of our eponymous "hero" when Nick returns home from his dinner with the Buchanans. Nick is out breathing the night air when he realizes that he is not alone: "fifty feet away a figure had emerged from the shadow of my neighbor's mansion and was standing with his hands in his pockets regarding the silver pepper of the stars." He is about to call to the stranger, but when he observes that the man is fixated by a faraway gleam of green light, he desists. And then the man who will be Gatsby is gone.

The first encounter, then, is with the fundamental mystery of Jay Gatsby. And for a time the mystery only grows. Nick starts seeing more of the Buchanans, and begins to date Daisy's friend, the cool but companionable Jordan Baker. Then he goes to one of Gatsby's legendary parties, which are, he eventually learns, nothing more than shimmering nets thrown out in the hopes of snaring Gatsby's long-lost love, Daisy. We see Gatsby as Nick sees him, magnified and dazzling in the strobe lights of rumor. They say he is a German spy, a nephew of Kaiser Wilhelm, a killer. A killer . . . against such opulence, the speculation about dark deeds is but a further exaltation of the image. The collective instinct is unerring: such a magnificent flower can only be sprung from an evil soil.

Gatsby is never more thrilling, more fantastic, than in those early, champagne-lit conjectures. Soon enough Nick will meet his neighbor and be drawn into his machinations. And though he will remain to the last an unknown quantity, Gatsby will slowly wither from episode to episode. After the mist of legend blows off, he becomes merely mysterious—a financier with peculiar connections, none more peculiar than his "gonnegtion" to Meyer Wolfsheim, the man who allegedly fixed the 1919 World Series. Then, when his quixotic obsession with Daisy is revealed, his mysteriousness is replaced by an aura of tragic pathos—Gatsby in love is as foolishly human as any of us.

Yet it is this love, the scale of it, that confers upon Gatsby whatever grandeur he finally possesses. Without it he is the Wizard of Oz—a behind-the-scenes operator with extensive ties to bootleggers and dubious financiers. When his dream of love is destroyed, he is nothing but his extravagant props—he is ready for George Wilson's bullet. In the end only his old father, Nick, and a few stragglers attend the funeral. And it is one of these stragglers, "the owl-eyed man," who gets the last word that day: "The poor son-of-a-bitch."

THE NOVEL ARGUES WITH ITSELF

On the surface, then, Fitzgerald has written a parable on the perennial American theme of outsized dreams and their bitter ruin. "I coulda been a contender," Brando says in *On the Waterfront.* In the last scene of *Death of a Salesman,* Charley sums things up for Biff. "Nobody dast blame this man. A salesman is got to dream, boy. It comes with the territory." And on and on. We do not have to work very hard to connect Fitzgerald's vision with the narrative of public life in our era—our Wall Street pirates, our stumping politicians looking for the light in the distance as they kick up the dust around their own suspect doings. Self-making is a bloody business. And Nick's awakening—"I wanted the world to be . . . at a sort of moral attention forever"—is ours.

But this parable of rise and fall, of magnificent mansions bought by dirty dealings, is not what determines *Gatsby*'s greatness or its ultimate relevance. That is only part of the picture. Indeed, running behind or beneath the obvious legend is a secondary narrative, a narrative that is less about paying the piper than it is about dreaming. About the power of our expectations and our longings. And it is the vibration that is set up when this presses against the ostensible plot that makes *Gatsby* so galvanizing—and so American. To put it simply, the novel argues with itself, and does so just as we do in our own souls. It purports to speak of incidents and moral consequences, but underneath it is communicating something much more ambiguous and suggestive.

First the sober opening:

> In my younger and more vulnerable years my father gave me some advice that I've been turning over in my mind ever since.

> "Whenever you feel like criticizing any one," he told me, "just remember that all the people in this world haven't had the advantages you've had."

Our narrator is going to give us a lesson, tell us a story about wising up—about coming to mature terms with human frailty. He is back from the East and Gatsby has fallen. But already by the fourth paragraph we sense that

Nick is at odds with himself. Directly after his claim that he wants "no more riotous excursions with privileged glimpses into the human heart," he introduces the name of Gatsby—Gatsby, who "represented everything for which I have an unaffected scorn," but in whom Nick had found "an extraordinary gift for hope, a romantic readiness such as I have never found in any other person and which it is not likely I shall ever find again."

This ambivalence is never really resolved. There is the tale, and there is the teller. And time and again we are given clues that the teller, our collective mouthpiece, that stand-up decent fellow from the Midwest, does not quite believe the tale—certainly not the lesson it would impart. The language repeatedly gives him away. Shrewd and cynical as he can be when characterizing the Buchanans or Jordan, he cannot get the note of reverence out of his voice when he writes of Gatsby and his gaudy displays. Here he notes the preparations for another of Gatsby's parties: "On buffet tables, garnished with glistening hors-d'oeuvre, spiced baked hams crowded against salads of harlequin designs and pastry pigs and turkeys bewitched to a dark gold." The prose—*glistening, harlequin, bewitched, dark gold*—is enraptured.

And the bacchanal itself? Again the tone and the rhythm inform on the observer:

> Laughter is easier minute by minute, spilled with prodigality, tipped out at a cheerful word. The groups change more swiftly, swell with new arrivals, dissolve and form in the same breath; already there are wanderers, confident girls who weave here and there among the stouter and more stable, become for a sharp, joyous moment the center of a group, and then, excited with triumph, glide on through the sea-change of faces and voices and color under the constantly changing light.

> Suddenly one of these gypsies, in trembling opal, seizes a cocktail out of the air, dumps it down for courage and, moving her hands like Frisco, dances out alone on the canvas platform.

If Nick is a man remembering scenes of past extravagance—the fireworks before the fall—then he has clearly been seduced by the promise all over again; against this indrawn breath of excitement any sober rectitude must feel willed.

THE MAGIC OF RENEWABILITY

Even after Gatsby has fallen to earth, after the dark secrets have come out, the lessons been grudgingly learned, Nick sustains a wistful yearning that the sad facts cannot destroy. Back in the Midwest, having survived to tell the tale, he reflects:

> West Egg, especially, still figures in my more fantastic dreams. I see it as a night scene by El Greco: a hundred houses, at once conventional and grotesque, crouching under a sullen, overhanging sky and a lustreless moon. In the foreground four solemn men in dress suits are walking along the sidewalk with a stretcher on which lies a drunken woman in a white evening dress. Her hand, which dangles over the side, sparkles cold with jewels. Gravely the men turn in at a house—the wrong house. But no one knows the woman's name, and no one cares.

It would be a despairing image, ought to be, except for the fascinated absorption of the narrating voice. Nick can't resist making his dream a *tour de force*, imparting to its staging a strange beauty.

None of this is incidental. Every cadenza, every perfectly orchestrated description, is part of the design, guiding the reader to the romantic surge of the book's final passages. These passages would surely strike us as excessive and overblown were they not most patiently prepared for. Step by step, mostly by way of the tone and the subliminal suggestiveness of the language, we have been made to recognize the true unconscious disposition of Nick's American soul. The man who began with both feet on the ground and his head screwed back on has unveiled the contrary side of his character. And it is the progress of this unveiling, its sudden final momentum, that imparts to *Gatsby* the magic of renewability.

The final passage is one of the best known in our literature, but I cite from it again.

> Most of the big shore places were closed now and there were hardly any lights except the shadowy, moving glow of a ferryboat across the Sound. And as the moon rose higher the inessential houses began to melt away until gradually I became aware of the old island here that flowered once for Dutch sailors' eyes—a fresh, green breast of the new world. Its vanished trees, the trees that had made way for Gatsby's house, had once pandered in whispers to the last and greatest of human dreams; for a transitory enchanted moment man must have held his breath in the presence of this continent, compelled into an aesthetic contemplation he neither understood nor desired, face to face for the last time in history with something commensurate to his capacity for wonder.

And

> Gatsby believed in the green light, the orgiastic future that year by year recedes before us. It eluded us then, but that's no

> matter—tomorrow we will run faster, stretch out our arms farther.... And one fine morning—
>
> So we beat on, boats against the current, borne back ceaselessly into the past.

This might well be the most lyrical patch of prose in our literature. Taken by itself it sounds florid, overwrought. There is only the last sentence, implacable beneath the lulling sway of its syllables, to mitigate the visionary excess. But encountering it as we do on the far side of Gatsby's exploded paradise, we are stirred at the deepest level. In a stroke Fitzgerald has forged the link between Gatsby's belief in love—the fabulous self-making enterprise it fostered—and the originating dream of the first European settlers. The mystery of this corrupt but also pathetic and forgivable man is seen as an attribute of something larger. As Nick says of Gatsby,

> He had come a long way to this blue lawn, and his dream must have seemed so close that he could hardly fail to grasp it. He did not know that it was already behind him, somewhere back in that vast obscurity beyond the city, where the dark fields of the republic rolled on under the night.

Nick has here restored to him the greatness of his desire. It is a desire that partakes of everything we feel when we consider our own fate, private and collective, under the larger dispensation, what the philosophers once called "the aspect of eternity." Insofar as we feel the inchoate promise of ourselves and our historical presence, we are joined to him.

A CLUE ABOUT RENEWAL

"So we beat on . . ." The boats are not defeated by the current—nothing so simple. They are "borne back ceaselessly into the past." And what is that past but the vision of those Dutch sailors, the imagining of a new history before which all other initiatives pale? If *The Great Gatsby* is indeed a cautionary tale, then it is really cautioning us against selling ourselves short, against turning in fear or disappointment from the lyrical call of our nature. Gatsby was not a fool for dreaming, only for not knowing how dreams intersect with realities.

Similarly, if *Gatsby* is a book for us today, it is not so in the obvious moralizing way. We are not asked to repudiate our more excessive selves. Rather, we are to recover in altered form something of the power of that intoxication, that amorous bent toward greater possibilities of feeling and action. Our basic excessiveness is not about greed or display, nor is it a frantic escape from the roll-call confinements of dailiness. It is a surviving trace of the awe that set everything into motion. And wounded and compromised as we may feel, there is a clue about renewal in that essential American image of dark fields rolling on under the night.

CHAPTER 3

Tender Is the Night

READINGS ON
E. SCOTT FITZGERALD

A Consistently Disturbing Novel

Brian Way

Tender Is the Night depicts the deterioration of a violent and hedonistic world, writes Brian Way, senior lecturer in English at University College, Swansea, England. The degeneration affects other characters but is concentrated in Dick Diver. It is important to understand the complex reasons behind Diver's decline, Way says; he charges that many critics unfairly accuse Fitzgerald of having been confused or ambiguous because he did not choose a single rationale for his character's degradation.

When D. W. Harding reviewed *Tender Is the Night* for *Scrutiny* in 1934, he used the word 'harrowing' to characterize its precise emotional tone. In the process of Dick Diver's deterioration, we feel the presence of unbearable pain, which is not relieved by any tragic catharsis. Although Harding in most ways failed to do justice to the novel's complexity and maturity, in this one respect he responded to it more sensitively than any other of Fitzgerald's critics. The harrowing quality of *Tender Is the Night* is remarkably consistent: it is concentrated in the figure of Dick Diver, but it is diffused through many other characters and incidents. There are almost infinite variations in the level of intensity, there are even apparent remissions, but it is never entirely absent.

There is, to begin with, a great deal of violence in *Tender Is the Night.* For the Divers and their friends, violence isn't confined to rare moments of personal conflict—it is part of the texture of everyday life. When Dick and Nicole go to the Gare St Lazare to see Abe North off to America, they become the casual witnesses of a murder. As the boat train is about to leave, an American woman takes a revolver out of her handbag and shoots her departing lover. 'Then, as if nothing had happened, the lives of the Divers and their friends

From *F. Scott Fitzgerald and the Art of Social Fiction* by Brian Way. Copyright © 1980 by Brian Way. Reprinted with permission of St. Martin's Press, Inc.

flowed out into the street.' The 'echoes of violence' which reverberate behind them are part of a hideous normality—like the condition of men at war. . . . Echoes of violence and the actuality of violence are a constant element in the atmosphere and structure of the novel. Even when the violence is farcical—in the duel between Tommy Barban and Albert McKisco, for instance, or in the scene where Gausse, the hotel proprietor, kicks Lady Caroline Sibly-Biers's bottom— it is a disturbing element. Often it is brutalizing and sordid, as it is in Dick's Roman brawl, or when Rosemary finds the body of the murdered negro, Peterson, casually dumped on her bed. Sometimes it is unspeakably horrible—the news of how Abe North was beaten to death in a New York speakeasy, which Dick hears being callously talked over in a Munich beer-cellar; and, above all, Devereux Warren's rape of his own daughter. The historical reverberations of the Great War . . . are a constant undertone to the lives of the individual characters. There is frequently, too, a sense of psychological violence, most obviously in the periodic outbreaks of Nicole's insanity, but most deeply in Dick's inner conflicts and the shocks inflicted on his sensibilities.

It is at this point that the echoes of violence are blended with other, no less disturbing, vibrations—the self-disgust, despair and mental anguish which so many of the characters feel. Fitzgerald's treatment of these states of feeling is at the farthest possible remove from the sort of *nostalgie de la boue* [longing for depravity] which is so tiresome a feature of, say, the existentialist novel. On the contrary, the surface of *Tender Is the Night* is urbane, polished, often beautifully serene: the horrors Fitzgerald's people experience are those which lurk beneath the most civilized and reassuring forms of existence. They are 'nice people', as Mary North explains to Dick in their last conversation—all they want is 'to have a good time'. And, if they are not having a good time in Paris or on the Riviera, they are in clinics and sanatoriums in Switzerland, being looked after in the best modern way. . . .

A COMPLEX DISINTEGRATION

There are many varieties of suffering and tension in *Tender Is the Night*, but all of them are subordinated in some degree to the case of Dick Diver—to the horror of watching a man who once possessed intellectual brilliance, moral integrity and charm, disintegrate slowly into an inert alcoholic wreck.

Even Nicole, who is not gifted with sympathy or understanding, grasps something of what is going on inside him as she watches him sitting alone on the terrace of their Riviera house. She is about to leave him—she has already become Tommy Barban's mistress—but she contemplates with some compunction the ruins of what she is leaving behind:

> He was thinking, he was living a world completely his own and in the small motions of his face, the brow raised or lowered, the eyes narrowed or widened, the lips set and reset, the play of his hands, she saw him progress from phase to phase of his own story spinning out inside him, his own, not hers. Once he clenched his fists and leaned forwards, once it brought into his face an expression of torment and despair— when this passed its stamp lingered in his eyes.

The most important thing to notice about Dick's deterioration is that it is not a simple process. The general failure to recognize this fact has had serious consequences for the reputation of *Tender Is the Night*: it has been subjected to a great deal of adverse criticism—most of it singularly inept—and to almost as much half-hearted praise. Critics have uneasily admitted, or loudly complained, that the novel is confused— that Fitzgerald was never clear in his own mind what caused Dick Diver's decline; that in consequence he told the story in the wrong order, and that even when Malcolm Cowley put it right for him after his death, it still didn't make sense. These critics usually proceed by selecting one of the possible explanations—that Dick is a victim of the rich, that his moral will is destroyed when he abandons his profession as a psychiatrist, that he exhausts himself emotionally by giving too much to other people—and then censure Fitzgerald for filling out the novel with false clues and irrelevant material. The conviction that it should be possible to isolate a single cause for so complex a change in personality, while it is intellectually absurd, faithfully reflects twentieth-century habits of thought. The rise of psychology and the social sciences has tended to give us a false sense of assurance in approaching human situations. Emboldened by spurious notions of scientific certainty, we are often led to claim for a single traumatic, environmental or historical factor the status of a complete explanation. The effect of these new sciences has been the contrary of what their greatest thinkers presumably intended: they have not refined our notions of human motivation but made them cruder. To be specific, they have created a climate of thought in which it is more difficult to read novels like *Tender Is the Night* intelligently.

Fitzgerald, by not succumbing to the temptation to schematize and simplify, takes his place in the best traditions of the art of fiction. It would not have seemed strange to the masters of classic European realism, nor presumably to their readers, that the deterioration of a human character—of, say, Tolstoy's Anna Karenina, or Stendhal's Julien Sorel, or George Eliot's Walter Lydgate—is not something to be summed up in a single confident formula. These novelists recognized that a multiplicity of factors contribute to the ruin of a human life and, in addition, they saw something which is possibly even more important: that a part of the horror of such situations is that they contain an element of mystery—beyond a certain point they are inexplicable.

Fitzgerald's treatment of Dick Diver has precisely this quality. *Tender Is the Night* is conceived on a scale which makes it possible for him to explore a human life in all its complexity and variety. It has an extraordinary richness and density of texture, so that the pattern of Dick Diver's inner life, the external facts of his career, the social pressures which bear down upon him, and the historical context within which he lives, are all given to us with minute and vivid particularity. At the same time, Fitzgerald conveys a sense of the mysterious, the unknowable, element in Dick's ruin—the things in him we can only guess at, as, like Nicole, we watch him sitting alone in his chair at the edge of the cliff. If the cumulative effect of the novel were not enough, Fitzgerald states the matter explicitly:

> He had lost himself—he could not tell the hour when, or the day or the week, the month or the year. Once he had cut through things, solving the most complicated equations as the simplest problems of his simplest patients. Between the time he found Nicole flowering under a stone on the Zurichsee and the moment of his meeting with Rosemary the spear had been blunted.

Dick's moment of self-analysis is interesting not only as a comment upon the process of his deterioration: it also contains the principle which underlies the structure of *Tender Is the Night.* If it is true that no single cause can be assigned to the break-up of a human personality, then it is also true that one cannot assign the deterioration to a particular moment in time—'he could not tell the hour when, or the day or the week, the month or the year'. This rules out the possibility of a simple chronological narrative, which only makes sense in the case of a character like Hurstwood in Theodore Dreiser's *Sister Carrie*. Hurstwood is the victim of a very simple equation of forces which push him down a kind of staircase one step at a time. For Dick Diver there is no simple equation of forces—in that sense there is no staircase to descend. . . .

A NAIVE AMERICAN OPTIMISM

Whatever else may be wrong with him, Dick is not in the ordinary sense a weak man—in fact, he almost always gives an impression of unusual strength. When one considers the pressures on him, it is astonishing that he lasts for so long. Even at the end, he has the capacity to endure and to obliterate himself without fuss—he comes out of the final showdown with Tommy Barban rather well.

Dick's cast of mind, however, makes him dangerously vulnerable. His habitual attitudes and favourite assumptions provide a poor basis for deciding how to live. This note is sounded at the beginning of his career by his Rumanian friend, who warns him, 'That's going to be your trouble—judgement about yourself.' Dick's sense of the balance between his own capabilities and limitations is clouded by a naive and rather presumptuous kind of American optimism—a feeling that he can become a great psychiatrist or even a complete man simply by an act of will. More seriously, he has a profound belief in the value of romantic failure—a view of the human situation which appealed to Fitzgerald from his earliest childhood. It must be said that Fitzgerald's attitude to this trait in Dick's character is highly equivocal: he does seem to imply that it is a reason for regarding the latter as a potentially heroic figure; on the other hand he is fully aware that there is something perverse in Dick's conviction that 'intactness' means 'incompleteness', and that, unless a man is 'a little damaged' by life, he remains forever unfulfilled. Dick's consequent tendency to take unnecessary risks, to match himself against impossible odds, certainly has much to do with his decision to marry Nicole. When he takes the case to his colleagues, Dr Dohmler and Franz Gregorovious, for their advice, the result is a foregone conclusion: Franz reminds him of what he knows already—that there is virtually no chance of building a happy marriage upon a mental patient's transference to her psychiatrist—while Dohmler doesn't find it necessary even to express an opinion on a question where the issues are so clear. Dick accepts their professional diagnosis, and at the same time ignores it: his love for Nicole is an overwhelming force, but, besides this, he is undoubtedly attracted by a situation in which defeat is almost inevitable. This is not merely the emotional basis for many of his most important choices: it is a conscious theory which he expounds, on occasion, with doctrinaire intensity. When Nicole complains, *à propos* of Abe North's alcoholism, that 'so many smart men go to pieces nowadays', Dick takes her up sharply: 'Smart men play close to the line because they have to—some of them can't stand it, and so they quit.'

Too Good a Writer to Make It Simple

[Dick Diver's] story assumes the dimensions of tragedy if one accepts his choice to marry Nicole and his choice to free her as deliberately made because of his love for her. But Fitzgerald is too good a writer to make it quite that simple. He is aware of the complexities of human motivations and personal relationships. He makes his character believable by showing the less admirable qualities in him and the selfish motives which complicate the altruistic.

Eugene White, *Modern Fiction Studies*, Spring 1961.

The pattern of Dick's mental processes exposes him to dangers no less great. Although his intellectual training is in the sciences, the basis of his thought is largely intuitive and imaginative, and the quality of these insights depends almost entirely on his emotional state at the time. On the afternoon of the shooting at the Gare St Lazare, he is prostrated by a nervous fatigue which is accentuated by his unhappiness over Rosemary. As he sits on a café terrace with her and Nicole, he finds that he has lost contact with them, has no sense of what they are thinking and feeling, no idea of how he might help them or even talk to them. Exhaustion turns him in upon himself, and deprives him of 'the long ground-swell of imagination that he counted on for his judgements'.

He carries these habits of mind into his scientific and clinical work with consequences that are generally disastrous. He relies too much upon his emotions to be a dependable psychiatrist. At times he exhausts himself by becoming over-involved in his patients—in the woman artist suffering from nervous eczema, and most of all, of course, in Nicole. At other times he cannot interest himself in his cases, and he is quite unable to deal with repellent people like the Australian family who precipitate his final departure from the clinic. He altogether lacks the quality of sympathetic detachment which a doctor needs in order to maintain his balance and his professional effectiveness. William Carlos Williams defines this special kind of humanity with unique precision in poems like 'Complaint' and 'The Injury', which draw upon his own medical experience. In the latter, the doctor participates in a sick man's struggle for breath, and yet a part of his mind is disengaged, free to observe other kinds of breathing—the panting of a freight locomotive in the nearby railroad yards, and the effortless song of a whitethroat at dawn.

A MAZE OF CORRUPTING COMPROMISES

Through his marriage, Dick condemns himself to a process of exhaustion. He gives himself extravagantly, and he is exploited: 'there was a pleasingness about him that simply had to be used.' In his relations with Nicole, he commits himself to an impossible set of conflicting demands: to being her husband and her psychiatrist; to conducting her through a series of gracious expatriate adventures, and at the same time continuing with his own scientific work; to becoming a pensioner of the American rich, and maintaining his personal independence. As the roles of lover and psychiatrist become inextricably confused, his confidence in his own professional judgement is progressively undermined. He gives up using hypnosis as a method of treatment because Nicole once laughed at his attempts to hypnotize her. At times the compulsive force of her psychosis threatens to engulf him: in the scene where she has one of her mad fits at a fairground, we are told that 'he could not watch her disintegrations without participating in them.' As a result, the Divers' marriage is not a mutually recreative relationship: Dick gets nothing in return for the enormous drain on his energies, and his affair with Rosemary is in part an acknowledgement of this fact. . . .

Through marrying Nicole, he finds himself entangled in a maze of compromises, a subtle process of corruption which undermines his moral will even more surely than the external pressures. With one part of himself he knows he must fight against the rich to preserve his own identity, but another, even stronger, side of his character drives him to compete with them, to try to beat them at their own game. His impulse to please, to charm, to entertain, and at the same time to dominate other people through a conscious use of these abilities, leads him to create a style, an aristocratic way of life, designed to surpass in its amenity and taste anything that the rich themselves are capable of. With the benefit of Rosemary's enraptured and uncritical gaze, we are able to do more than justice to the beautiful surface of the Divers' existence. When she joins them for a morning swim, she finds that it is no ordinary swim but a carefully arranged hedonistic adventure. They move 'from the heat to the cool with the gourmandise of a tingling curry eaten with a chilled white wine. The Divers' day was spaced like the day of the older civilizations to yield the utmost from the materials at hand, and to give all the transitions their full value.' The dinner at the Villa Diana affects Rosemary even more deeply: the table itself seems to her to rise a little towards the sky in response to the powerful enchantment of Dick's charm.

Even in these beatific moments at the very beginning of the novel, Fitzgerald hints at disturbing undercurrents of which Rosemary is unaware. During the beach scene from which I have just quoted, he qualifies her enthusiasm with some severity:

> Her naiveté responded whole-heartedly to the expensive simplicity of the Divers, unaware of its complexity and its lack of innocence, unaware that it was all a selection of quality rather than quantity from the run of the world's bazaar; and that the simplicity of behaviour also, the nursery-like peace and good will, the emphasis on the simpler virtues, was part of a desperate bargain with the gods and had been attained through struggles she could not have guessed at. At that moment the Divers represented externally the exact furthermost evolution of a class, so that most people seemed awkward beside them—in reality a qualitative change had already set in that was not at all apparent to Rosemary. . . .

A KEY ELEMENT OF MORAL CHAOS

Fitzgerald's conflicting feelings about what is desirable in human life are reflected most clearly in his sense of class. All the colour, excitement and beauty of existence are associated in his mind with the idea of an aristocracy. Even in

Tender Is the Night, for all its pessimism, there are haunting intimations of what might have been realized—moments on Gausse's beach, in the gardens of the Villa Diana, and in the streets and cafés of Paris.

In opposition to this, there is a provincial, puritanical, middle-class midwesterner in Fitzgerald, who not only scrutinizes the short-comings of the rich with uncompromising rigour, but finds the firmest moral ground in a version of the middle-class protestant ethic. Dick Diver's sense of dedication to the profession of medicine and to scientific discovery at the outset of his career can be seen only in these terms; his sense of morality is an extension of the ethics of his profession. Of all the acts of self-betrayal which contribute to his ruin, the abandonment of his proper work is probably the most serious in its effects. This is a largely unconscious process—a succession of compromises and equivocations which carry him insidiously into deeper and deeper moral confusion. Fitzgerald describes a significant stage in the process when he shows Dick returning to work after the first phase of his adventure with Rosemary is over. Dick's work-room is, to all appearances, a little temple of the sciences—a cottage in the grounds of the Villa Diana, well away from the house itself. Its shutters are closed against the glare, and no servant is ever allowed inside for fear of disturbing the 'ordered confusion' of his piles of notes. He takes stock of the vast research project which has occupied his mind for many years, and, without being aware of the full implications of what he is doing, in effect abandons it. Through a series of subtle rationalizations, he persuades himself that it would be better to summarize his ideas in a short book which he could finish quickly. He is stimulated by the feeling that he has put his thoughts in order, and the same impulse leads him to clean and tidy up his room. He rearranges his notes, sweeps the floor, disinfects his washroom, sends away for new books. Then, more than satisfied with his afternoon's work, he takes a modest drink of gin.

Fitzgerald's insight into the psychology of subtle evasion and self-deception here is incomparably sensitive and precise. He has been praised for many things, but the lucidity of perception and the sober penetrating intelligence, which are so evident in this and scores of other places in *Tender Is the Night*, have never been adequately recognized. In this brilliantly observed little scene, we see how the manner of

Dick's new life has gradually come to supplant the substance of the old. There is no sense here of real scientific work being done: the ritual of privacy and academic seclusion, the obligatory gestures which supposedly accompany deep thought, are mere play-acting, a charade as empty as the performances of Dick's social life—as meaningless as the games he plays to amuse and captivate the little circle on Gausse's beach. This game, however, is one he plays alone: the only audience it can possibly dazzle and bewitch is Dick himself. It is only much later, when the experiment of running a psychiatric clinic in partnership with Franz has also failed, that he grasps fully what has been happening to him: 'Not without desperation he had long felt the ethics of his profession dissolving into a lifeless mass'.

Dick's case is not an isolated one—indeed Fitzgerald sees it as in many ways typical of the age. *Tender Is the Night* is, among other things, a historical novel, one which seeks not only to evoke the unique character of a particular period in time, but, in Georg Lukács' phrase, to trace 'the pre-history of the present' to turn to the immediate past for some of the evidence needed to understand what is happening now. For Fitzgerald, it was the existence of the professions, and of the exacting sense of responsibility they embodied, which alone ensured the health of the nineteenth-century middle-class civilization he so much admired. It is therefore not surprising that Fitzgerald should regard the undermining of professional ethics as a key element in the moral chaos of the postwar decade. . . .

Fitzgerald's success in *Tender Is the Night* is no less complete than in *The Great Gatsby*. Almost all the criticism of his work has been bedevilled by the attempt to elevate the reputation of one novel at the expense of the other—a foolish proceeding, which has been a serious obstacle to the proper appreciation of his work. As he himself recognized, the two novels exemplify quite distinct approaches to the art of fiction: *Gatsby* uses the method of poetic concentration which Henry James—more than anyone else within the American tradition—had developed; *Tender Is the Night* has the extended scope and the richness of detail which one associates with classic European realism. In both novels, Fitzgerald is equally successful in achieving complexity of meaning and artistic truth.

Tender Is the Night and Hollywood

Aaron Latham

Aaron Latham's research for his Princeton dissertation on Fitzgerald's movie career led to his book *Crazy Sundays,* from which this article is excerpted. Latham describes Fitzgerald's collaboration on *Tender Is the Night* with seventeen-year-old Bill Warren, who, like the young Fitzgerald, was writing and producing musicals when they met. When the novel, published during the depression, failed to sell well, Fitzgerald became interested in turning the novel into a screenplay, because sales to the movie industry were still high. Although Fitzgerald and Warren could interest no studio in their script, twenty-two years after Fitzgerald died, *Tender Is the Night*—the movie—was released by 20th Century–Fox.

It was four o'clock in the morning when Bill Warren's phone rang.

"Get over here and straighten this out," said a man with a thick voice at the other end. He meant straighten out *Tender Is the Night.*

The seventeen-year-old never protested. He dressed in his dark Baltimore home at 605 North Charles Street, then headed for 1307 Park Avenue. He found the author standing at a high, old-fashioned desk. Scott had taken to doing all his writing on his feet, but if this eccentricity made him look like a pastor at his pulpit, he was one with liquor on his breath. Bill walked over and stood beside him, and they both looked down at the new pages covered with handwriting which could not walk a straight line. "He wanted me to make sense out of what he had written," Warren remembers, "but sometimes I couldn't even figure out the words."

From *Crazy Sundays: F. Scott Fitzgerald in Hollywood* by Aaron Latham. Copyright © 1970, 1971 by John Aaron Latham. Used by permission of Viking Penguin, a division of Penguin Books USA Inc.

Bill went to work editing, rewriting, changing, while Scott looked on, growing more and more impatient. The boy crossed out "he expostulated" and wrote in "he said." Scott put his arm around Bill, whom he had already taken as his godson.

"Don't change that," he said. "That's why I'm who I am. Who the hell are you?"

The unpublished beginner and the recognized author had the same argument almost every day. "I always thought that dialogue was very well contained if you used 'he said,' 'she said,'" Warren explains. "Scott would write, 'he expostulated,' 'he ejaculated,' '"Ah," he complained.'"

When they weren't fighting about how to write dialogue, they fought about how to open chapters. "Scott always wanted to begin chapters with 'The moon shone thinly over the city,'" Warren remembers. "I would begin, 'The trains from the South arrived three times a day. She was on one of them.'"

"How dare you rewrite me?" was Fitzgerald's standard protest. "How do you know the trains arrived three times a day?"

Warren had an answer: "You told me." . . .

A STORY ABOUT THE MOVIES

Fitzgerald had begun *Tender Is the Night* in France eight years before, when Bill Warren was nine years old and Zelda was whole. No mental illness clouded those first drafts: the novel was originally conceived as a story about the movies. Scott called his hero Francis Melarky, made him a motion-picture cameraman, and placed him in Europe.

At first Francis is bored with the whole expatriate merry-go-round. Then he discovers that Earl Brady has come over and is making a picture in Monte Carlo. Tired of doing nothing, Francis drives to Brady's studio, a little Hollywood marooned on the Riviera, where he hopes to get back into pictures. Making his way across a darkened stage, Francis notices (as George Hanaford in Fitzerald's story "Magnetism" and Rosemary Hoyt in *Tender* would after him) that "here and there figure spotted the twilight, figures that turned up ashen faces to him, like souls in purgatory watching the passage of a mortal through." When the unemployed cameraman finally finds the man he is looking for, the director Brady, he stands in the shadow watching him work, and is thrown "into a sympathetic and approving trance." Soon Francis, like Gatsby, begins to dream, but he dreams not of a girl like Daisy, nor of a green light across the bay. His dreams are movie dreams:

> More than anything in the world he wanted to make pictures. He knew exactly what it was like to carry a picture in his head as a director did and it seemed to him infinitely roman- tic. Watching, he felt simply enormous promise, an unrolling of infinite possibilities in himself. He felt closer to Brady, murmuring on in his quiet deep-seated voice, than he had to anyone for months.

Moved by his desire to make movies, Francis goes up to Brady and introduces himself. Brady remembers the young cameraman from Hollywood and so offers him some back- handed flattery. "You've got ideas," the producer says. "You're sort of a stimulating kid. Take for instance authors—I've never been able to use their God damn stories, but I kept bringing them out to the coast because they're stimulating to have around." Fitzgerald, who would soon be on his way to the coast to write *Lipstick,* could not have known how prophetic these words would prove to be.

When Francis tells his mother—whom he was to kill later in the story—that he plans a comeback as a cameraman, she reminds her son:

> "You told me all they did was make you wait. You said you sat around one whole morning waiting."
> "I did say that, but I explained to you that waiting is just part of the picture business. Everybody's so much overpaid that when something finally happens you realize that you were making money all the time. The reason it's slow is be- cause one man's keeping it all in his head, and fighting the weather and the accidents—"
> "Let's not go over all that again, dear."

Even before his trip to Hollywood, Fitzgerald already knew what kind of world he would find there. . . .

Brushing aside his mother's worries, Francis jumps back into pictures. Like his creator, Francis had been away from his art for a long time, but thanks to Brady he sees his di- rection once again—just as Fitzgerald, writing the story, must have thought that he saw his:

> Walking out on the beach for a swim before dinner, Francis evoked from the day's hope and from the health in his brown- ing body, a robust old thought that work was more fun than anything. He felt that he was a good man and could do things no one else could. The few strangers left on the beach real-

ized this and swaying together clinked glasses to him. "Hurray for Francis Melarky!" He resolved to cut out the beer he drank with his meals, for how could he be at his best when he was short-winded? On the other hand, so he thought perversely, if he became an athlete in perfect trim, how could he respond to such toasts as they had just given him here? To achieve and to enjoy, to be prodigal and openhearted and yet ambitious and wise, to be strong and self-controlled, yet to miss nothing—to do and yet to symbolize . . . to be both light and dark.

In articulating the aspiring young movie maker's dilemma—*to do and yet symbolize*—Fitzgerald had set down his own. On the one hand he wanted to prove that he was a better writer "than any of the young Americans *without exception.*" On the other hand he wanted to have more fun than anyone else in France. He even took time away from his novel to try to become the man he was writing about—time to sight through a whirring camera, time to make an amateur film. . . .

THE TRANSFORMATIONS BEGIN

When Fitzgerald was not playing cameraman himself, he went on with his story of Francis Melarky, but as he wrote, his hero began to twist beneath his pencil. "About this time a change began to come over Francis," Fitzgerald put down. "He began to see himself as a more powerful person. . . . The symbol of his power became Earl [Brady]." Francis wanted a director's privileges not only at the studio but in society; he began to believe that "it needed only a word from him to change entire relations." To detach a wife from a husband would be as easy as ordering an actress to walk across the stage, or so Francis believed, and he set out to prove that he was right.

As important as the change which came over Francis, however, was a change coming over Fitzgerald himself. Once he became preoccupied with a director—once the director became for him "the symbol of . . . power"—the author began to lose interest in Francis. Why write a story about a man who ran a camera when he could write about a man who ran the whole show? The year was probably 1927, a time for upheavals. Francis Melarky, like the silent movies, was about to be replaced.

At this point, Fitzgerald broke off working on the Melarky story. Perhaps he, like Francis, felt that "more than anything in the world he wanted to make pictures," so he took a job in Hollywood. The result was *Lipstick.* Failing to strike gold in California, the author left the West and moved to Ellerslie, just outside Wilmington, Delaware, where he took up his novel again, but he did not take it up where he had left off. Rather, he decided to scrap Francis and start over. This time he chose as his hero Lew Kelly, a brilliant young director of motion pictures. Kelly's mind was described as "made up of all tawdry souvenirs of his time, things given away, unearned, like the pictures of celebrities he had once collected from cigarette packages. Somewhere in the littered five-and-ten glowed the low, painful fire of his talent." We are first introduced to Kelly and his wife Nicole on board a ship bound for Europe. A young actress named Rosemary is also making the crossing. Her ambitious mother persuades her to sneak across from tourist class into first class so that she can meet the prominent movie maker. In this early version of the story, she is literally looking for a director. In the final version, she would find her director, symbolically, in Dick Diver.

In 1931 the author decided to make his second raid on Hollywood. His script for *The Redheaded Woman,* of course, failed to make his fortune; banished from Metro, he headed back east and back to his novel. He rented a house in Baltimore and there, far from the Riviera, took up the story of his American expatriates.

A COLLABORATION BEGINS

Charles Marquis (Bill) Warren met Scott Fitzgerald in Baltimore's Vagabond Theatre. "I was doing a musical called *So What* with Gary Moore," Warren remembers. "I had written the book and the music. We were rehearsing one afternoon very late—all of the chorus girls and skit girls had gone home. I was at the piano playing 'Our Life Will Be a Wow' and telling this one girl to make the song light, airy, when out of the dark came this great big fedora. I saw a man dressed for winter, overcoat and all, and here it was the dead of summer. The man introduced himself and said, 'I'd like to work with you.' With youth's arrogance, I thought, 'Who the hell wouldn't?' When he left, everyone asked me, 'Do you know who that was?' But I didn't know F. Scott Fitzgerald. Hell, I didn't know Ernest Hemingway. I was a fast seventeen. After I found out that he wasn't a ragpicker, no matter what he dressed like, I went to see him." . . .

During those years Zelda was in and out of the Shepherd Pratt Clinic. . . . She was teaching Scott lessons about tragedy which Aristotle had left out. He retained the young actress Rosemary in his story, but changed his hero from a director to a doctor. The doctor, however, was to be something of a showman. He was not descended from actor George Hanaford ("Magnetism"), cameraman Melarky, and director Kelly for nothing.

Warren worked with Fitzgerald on the final drafts of *Tender Is the Night*, then they collaborated on a motion-picture treatment of the novel. Some days Bill simply acted as a kind of stenographer. Other days he would take pages covered with Scott's sprawling handwriting, sit down with a legal pad, and rewrite whole scenes. He remembers especially the shooting episode at the railroad station in Paris, which he reworked, trying to give it a more dramatic structure. In recognition of Bill's efforts, Scott put him in the book: the author named Nicole's father Charles Marquis Warren in the first edition of the novel, then changed it to Devereux Warren in later printings. "It was our hidden symbol," remembers the man who gave his name.

"If I tell you that I wrote part of *Tender Is the Night*, then you'll tell me that you wrote *The Sun Also Rises*," says Warren. But when the novel was published, eight years after it was begun, Fitzgerald inscribed a copy to his "godson" as follows: "For Charles (Bill) Warren with the hope that our co-operation will show us to prosperity. April 1st (fool's day 1934)." . . .

IF YOU CAN'T BEAT 'EM . . .

In 1934, when *Tender Is the Night* appeared in the bookstores, the Depression was hurting book sales much more than the picture business. A few farmers might escape the Oklahoma Dust Bowl by piling into an old Ford and heading for California, but most Americans sought escape from hard times by piling into movie houses. They lost themselves in films like John Ford's *Lost Patrol*; went to Frank Capra's *It Happened One Night* to see long-legged Claudette Colbert trounce Clark Gable in a hitchhiking contest; fell in love with the man who hated dogs and small children, old bulb-nosed W.C. Fields, star of *It's a Gift*. That was stern competition, especially for a book like Fitzgerald's which offered no refuge—a book which was, in fact, about deterioration. *Tender Is the Night* sold only thirteen thousand copies—*This Side of Paradise* had sold twice as many the first week—and left Fitzgerald in financial quicksand.

It did not take long for Scott to see that the lines were forming in front of the theatres, not the bookstalls, and so once again he began to think about show business. After all, the movies had haunted the author and his novel ever since those early chapters about Francis Melarky, the man who wanted to make movies more than anything. Scott decided that he and Warren should write a movie treatment of *Tender Is the Night* which they would sell to Hollywood. . . .

"Scott didn't know anything about adaptations," Warren says. The *Tender Is the Night* which the author and his young collaborator knocked out in a few weeks for the screen was very different from the novel which had cost eight years. . . . For example, in the book Nicole has been raped by her father, a rich capitalist, and his act becomes a metaphor for capitalism's original sin; the "winding mossy ways"[1] of her own mind become her purgatory as she atones for her father's guilt by going insane. In the movie treatment she simply gets a bump on the head. . . .

When the movie treatment was finished, Fitzgerald staked his collaborator to a trip to Hollywood. Scott hoped that Warren, besides selling himself to the studios, might be able to sell *Tender Is the Night*. Fitzgerald gave Warren several letters of introduction which were supposed to unlock the movie world for him. . . .

Soon Warren was sending Fitzgerald letters from the coast. One informed Scott: "Your name is big and hellishly well known in the studios. You rate out here as a highbrow writer but you rate as a thoroughbred novelist and not a talkie hack and therefore these people look up to you." The letter went on to suggest, however, that being looked up to was no way to get rich. "Lower your highbrow & help on some trash," he advised the author of *The Great Gatsby* and *Tender Is the Night*. "They buy trash here—they're quite willing to pay high for it. . . . If you would forget originality and finesse and think in terms of cheap melo theatrics you would probably have made a howling success of your visits here and would likewise have no financial worries now." (Much later, Warren would follow his own ad-

---

1. John Keats, "Ode to a Nightingale," quoted on the title page of *Tender Is the Night*

vice and create the world's most successful television show, *Gunsmoke*.) . . .

Despite his high hopes and fine understanding of melo Hollywood, Bill Warren could not find a studio job or interest anyone in *Tender Is the Night*; he returned to New York and went to work writing detective stories for the pulps. Fitzgerald wrote Maxwell Perkins that "for a whole year" he had hoped for a financial "break in the shape of either Hollywood buying *Tender* or else . . . getting . . . someone else to do an efficient dramatization." But the break had not come and the author thought that he knew why.

> I know I would not like the job, and I know that [Owen] Davis who had every reason to undertake it after the success of [his Broadway version of] *Gatsby* simply turned thumbs down from his dramatist's instinct that the story was not constructed as dramatically as *Gatsby* and did not readily lend itself to dramatization.

Perhaps Fitzgerald was remembering the problems he had had turning *Tender Is the Night* into a movie when he wrote in a short story called "Financing Finnegan":

> It was only when I met some poor devil of a screenwriter who had been trying to make a logical story out of one of his books that I realized he had his enemies.

> "It's all beautiful when you read it," this man said disgustedly, "but when you write it down plain it's like a week in the nuthouse."

BYPASSING BROADWAY

. . . In 1938 a New York dramatist named Mrs. Edwin Jarrett wrote a dramatic version of *Tender Is the Night* which she hoped to see staged on Broadway. A carbon of her adaptation reached Fitzgerald in Hollywood shortly after a producer had rewritten a screenplay on which Scott had worked for months. "I want especially to congratulate you," Scott wrote Mrs. Jarrett, ". . . on the multiple feats of ingenuity with which you've handled the difficult geography and chronology so that it has a unity which, God help me, I wasn't able to give it." Fitzgerald worried, however, about the handling of Dick Diver in the play. "I did not manage, I think in retrospect, to give Dick the cohesion I aimed at," the author confessed, "but in your dramatic interpretation I beg you to guard me from the exposal of this. I wonder what the hell the first actor who played Hamlet thought of the part? I can hear him say, 'The guy's a nut, isn't he?' (We can always find great consolation in Shakespeare.)" Fitzgerald noted that the play would have to "get by Broadway first," but if it did, he assured the playwright that Robert Montgomery wanted to play Dick Diver in a film version. But the play never did get by Broadway—it never even got to it.

It was not until 1962, twenty-two years after Fitzgerald died a Hollywood failure, that his novel was finally made into a movie. It was released by 20th Century–Fox, for whom the author had once worked (they had fired him after a few weeks).

Psychiatry: Zelda and Dick Diver

Frederick J. Hoffman

After briefly tracing the stages *Tender Is the Night*
went through during the nine years it took Fitzgerald to write it, author and English professor Frederick J. Hoffman connects the decision to make the
protagonist a psychiatrist to Zelda Fitzgerald's mental breakdowns, which began in 1930. (Zelda was
eventually diagnosed with incurable schizophrenia.)
Hoffman links the ironies of Diver's downfall to
Fitzgerald's own state of self-realization as Zelda's
condition deteriorated.

F. Scott Fitzgerald's *Tender Is the Night* (1934) is interesting
not only for what it contains in itself but for the history of its
composition. It came at the beginning of what proved to be
the second half of his career. Already solidly established as
an important writer through the publication in 1925 of *The
Great Gatsby* and a popular one since the "early success" of
This Side of Paradise (1920), Fitzgerald began planning for
his most ambitious work in 1925. He spent nine years puz-
zling over the form it should take, writing preliminary
sketches, changing and shifting his characters and scenes.
At various times the novel (or its preliminary versions) carried one of these titles: *The Boy Who Killed His Mother, The
Melarkey Case, Doctor Diver's Holiday, The Doctor's Holiday,
Our Type, World's Fair,* and finally *Tender Is the Night.*

The changes were not all a consequence of Fitzgerald's inability to decide upon a useful form. These were years of extreme trial for the Fitzgeralds. They seemed first of all determined to live up to their reputations; they competed with
each other for recognition; and Zelda Fitzgerald began to
show the consequences of the pace she had set for herself
and for her husband. For the first time in his life, psychiatry

became an absorbing and necessary world of discourse. The fortunes of the Fitzgeralds varied as Zelda's health improved or declined. Fitzgerald was forced to judge the world of his fiction from a new point of view. He had already presented that world, with its confusion, its moral chaos, its suggestions of imminent violence, from the perspective of the sensitive artist he occasionally proved he could be. But while his fiction often suggested psychoanalytic situations, easily accessible to the interpretations of analysis, he had seldom considered psychoanalysis itself, either as a frame of reference or as a *modus operandi*. Now, as Zelda's troubles demanded more and more of his time, and he turned to the texts of psychoanalysis from necessity and to satisfy his curiosity, he began to reconsider the plans of his new novel and to give dramatic emphasis to both the science of psychiatry and the lives and work of psychiatrists.[1]

Malcolm Cowley, in his excellent editing of the final version of *Tender Is the Night,*[2] suggests three separate developments in its planning and composition. The first, the "Melarkey version" (begun on the Riviera, late summer of 1925) was supposed to feature a young Hollywood technician, Francis Melarkey, who "would fall in love with a woman like Nicole Diver, would go on too many wild parties, would lose control of himself, and would kill his mother in a fit of rage." This plan scarcely resembles the 1934 novel. In the second or "Rosemary version" (written about 1929–1930) Melarkey has disappeared, or has dissolved into three Hollywood characters: Lewellen Kelly, a famous motion-picture director who is taking his wife Nicole to Europe for a vacation; and "Rosemary," who tries to attract his attention in the hope of getting a screen test. In the 1934 novel, Kelly and his

1. Zelda's first breakdown occurred April 23, 1930. Fitzgerald took her to Montreux, Switzerland, for examination; the diagnosis was schizophrenia. At the end of January, 1931, the Fitzgeralds were in the United States when Zelda suffered her second collapse and was taken to Baltimore for treatment. Shortly thereafter she sent to Maxwell Perkins of Scribner's the manuscript of her novel, *Save Me the Waltz,* which she had written in six weeks, mostly during her stay in the hospital. The novel is essentially an attack upon her husband and a self-justification of her own ambition to become a ballet dancer, a plan which Fitzgerald had opposed or at least made difficult of achievement. In December, 1933, she suffered a third breakdown and was returned to the hospital in Baltimore in what appeared to be an incurable state. Throughout these experiences, Fitzgerald was haunted by a sense of guilt; and, although the doctors assured him that the basic cause dated from a time long before he had first met her, he rightly suspected that the years of wildly confused living—in New York, Paris, Hollywood, the Riviera—had much to do with bringing on the several stages of her collapse. See Arthur Mizener, *The Far Side of Paradise* (Boston, 1951).
2. The following discussion is based upon Cowley's examination of manuscripts at The Princeton University Library.

wife become Dick and Nicole Diver, the association with Hollywood dropped altogether; Rosemary becomes an accomplished child star, who with her mother is on vacation in Europe as the completed novel begins.

A CHANGE OF EMPHASIS, NOT THEME

The third and final version, the "Dick Diver version," was begun early in 1932 and became the finished form of the 1934 novel. Here the hero is a promising young psychiatrist. It is obvious that the events of 1930 and 1931 influenced this new development profoundly. Summing up the variations, Cowley suggests that the essential theme of the three versions is that of "an ambitious young American [who] goes to Europe and is ruined by his contact with the leisure class." The leisure class was the focus at the beginning, as it continued to be, though with modifications, to the end. The most important change of emphasis came when Fitzgerald decided that the hero-victim-judge should be, not a Hollywood technician or director, but a psychiatrist. In this change the novel became a significant addition to the modern evaluation of the social and human comedies. That he thought this to be the most important fact of the novel is evident from a letter to Maxwell Perkins (1938): "[The novel's] great fault is that the *true* beginning—the young psychiatrist in Switzerland—is tacked away in the middle of the book." Fitzgerald then proposed taking the section of the 1934 edition which considers Diver's beginnings and his meeting with Nicole Warren and starting the novel with it. The 1934 beginning, which features the point of view of Rosemary Hoyt, would thus be moved back and Dick Diver would gain new prominence as the novel's hero.[3]

THE ILLUSIONS OF THE FITZGERALD HERO

At age 26, in the spring of 1917, Dick Diver arrives in Zurich, his entire, promising career ahead of him. It is important to see that he is not just a young psychiatrist, that he has the

3. Cowley followed Fitzgerald's wish almost to the letter in the volume prepared for the 1951 edition. See his introduction to that edition for the details. Concerning the *effect* of the changes, Cowley has this to say: "By rearranging the story in chronological order Fitzgerald tied it together. He sacrificed a brilliant beginning and all the element of mystery, but there is no escaping the judgment that he ended with a better constructed and more effective novel." (xiv–xv) There is much to be said for the 1934 arrangement, and it is doubtful that the psychiatric problem is better seen by bringing it up front. In any event, it seems to me that the point of view of Rosemary Hoyt, as it is given in the 1934 version, gives one a more vivid sense of the essential issue of the novel, of which the psychiatry is after all a form of judgment and appraisal rather than its substance.

mark of the Fitzgerald hero upon him. "Dick got up to Zurich on less Achilles' heels than would be required to equip a centipede, but with plenty—the illusions of eternal strength and health, and of the essential goodness of people; illusions of a nation, the lies of generations of frontier mothers who had to croon falsely that there were no wolves outside the cabin door." However inexpertly put here, the illusions are strictly needed for the development and collapse of the Fitzgerald hero. He is a man of great promise, charm, earnestness, balanced against a destructive naïveté. *Tender Is the Night* is far more an account of illusions clumsily and pathetically supported than it is a psychiatric appraisal of modern ills. The source of Nicole's illness is in its own way like the source of Dick's ambition. The group of expatriates who are attracted to the Diver world are also in one way or another affected by that combination of naïve hope and neurasthenic despair which characterizes so many of Fitzgerald's personages. The psychiatry is therefore not so much a judgment upon this world as it is an explanation of it. In the life of the Warrens the extreme forms of this confusion are realized. Their basis is wealth—or rather, extraordinary and powerful and wasteful substance, which sponsors and permits indulgences that drive irresponsible persons to disaster. Fitzgerald's analysis of the Warren money involves one in the full range of the novel's meaning; one phase of it is to be found reflected in the image of the 18-year-old movie star, Rosemary Hoyt, and her latest "Daddy's Girl" role:

> There she was—the school girl of a year ago, hair down her back and rippling out stiffly like the solid hair of a tanagra figure; there she was—*so* young and innocent—the product of her mother's loving care; there she was—embodying all the immaturity of the race, cutting a new cardboard paper doll to pass before its empty harlot's mind.

The "Daddy's Girl" motif reflects the causes of Nicole Warren's original disorder. Here, in Rosemary's depiction of the "sweetest thing's" vacuous sweetness, we have superficially the criticism of a low level of public taste, but it has also a suggestion of confused morality and basically an ignorance of matters that it is disastrous not to know about the human psychic economy. Another aspect of Fitzgerald's indictment of the American scene (or the Warren phase of it) has to do with the preposterous idea that money confers privilege, mobility, and a beyond-good-and-evil moral ad-

WHY DICK DIVER MEETS HIS DOOM

The central figure of *Tender Is the Night* is Dick Diver, a psychiatrist who, one can't help noticing, is singularly unable to diagnose his own psychic ills. The book charts Diver's course downward from professional promise and personal happiness to utter obscurity and moral decay. The reader's last glimpses of Diver find him moving to smaller and smaller towns in upstate New York; rumor has it that his last move was occasioned by an unpleasant affair he had with one of his patients. . . .

It is Nicole, first Diver's patient and then his wife, who brings about his confrontation with great wealth and who is the agent of his decline. Her fortune is ever swelling, and as news of its increase is brought, throughout the novel, by one character or another, one comes to feel that money is the dynamic, inexorable force that drives Diver downward. He has no power over these matters. Not only does he lack the strength to give his life a purpose in the face of such wealth, but he is also unable to free himself from its enervating effects after Nicole has left him.

Diver acts as though he had been created without any will at all. Consequently it is virtually impossible to make any sort of moral evaluation of Diver's actions. He has been destroyed by forces he could neither control nor even fully understand, and the moral judgment he had once possessed was of no use.

The fate of Dick Diver furnishes insight into Fitzgerald's later moralism and the nature of his contrition for past sins. To him it was believable that a man should lose his zest for work, his desire to make any contribution to society, if the profit motive is removed. And without work a man's character crumbles. This begins to sound remarkably like the Protestant ethic. If profit is, then, to some extent the measure of virtue, the fact that Fitzgerald's writing didn't sell served to aggravate the frustrations of his other personal adversities. It increased his sense of guilt without increasing his understanding.

Kent and Gretchen Kreuter, "The Moralism of the Later Fitzgerald," in *Modern Fiction Sudies*, VII (Spring 1961).

vantage. "Baby" Warren, Nicole's older sister, believes in the doctrine: *their* money will buy anything and everything; it will above all purchase a physician-husband for Nicole, and love need not be considered in the arrangement. Fitzgerald portrays this Warren offense as an atro-

cious violation of moral taste, whose efficiency makes it all
the more menacing.

> Nicole was the product of much ingenuity and toil. For her
> sake trains began their run at Chicago and traversed the
> round belly of the continent to California; chicle factories
> fumed and link belts grew link by link in factories; men
> mixed toothpaste in vats and drew mouthwash out of copper
> hogsheads; girls canned tomatoes quickly in August or
> worked rudely at the Five-and-Tens on Christmas Eve . . .
> these were some of the people who gave a tithe to Nicole, and
> as the whole system swayed and thundered onward it lent a
> feverish bloom to such processes of hers as wholesale buy-
> ing, like the flush of a fireman's face holding his post before
> a spreading blaze. She illustrated very simple principles, con-
> taining in herself her own doom, but illustrated them so ac-
> curately that there was grace in the procedure, and presently
> Rosemary would try to imitate it.

This is obviously a "case for the psychoanalyst," but Fitzgerald made it a matter of social case study. The applications of
psychoanalysis are imperfect, certainly not strictly accurate;
they need to extend beyond the limits of Nicole's illness, to
embrace the whole society of a people who for a decade
wanted only to be entertained. Specifically, the novel exploits
the dramatic possibilities of a transference-love situation.
Diver, asked by his friend to help in the case of the wealthy
American patient, finds that she has easily fallen in love with
him; and, while he is aware of the risks in the situation, is
half-inclined to return the love. In a conversation with two
colleagues, Diver confesses his perplexity and fear:

> Again Franz tried to speak—again Dohmler stopped
> him with a question directed pointedly at Dick. "Have you
> thought of going away?"
> "I can't go away."
> Doctor Dohmler turned to Franz: "Then we can send
> Miss Warren away."
> "As you think best, Professor Dohmler," Dick conceded.
> "It's certainly a situation."
> Professor Dohmler raised himself like a legless man
> mounting a pair of crutches.
> "But it is a professional situation," he cried quietly.
>
> •   •   •   •   •   •   •
>
> "I'm half in love with her—the question of marrying
> her has passed through my mind."
> "Tch! Tch!" uttered Franz.
> "Wait," Dohmler warned him. Franz refused to wait:
> "What! And devote half your life to being doctor and nurse and
> all—never! I know what these cases are. One time in twenty
> it's finished in the first push—better never see her again!"

THE DECLINE AND FALL OF DICK DIVER

But Diver does eventually give in, does hope that the "professional situation" can somehow be translated without harm into a personal situation. Throughout "Baby" Warren thinks of her sister's husband as a hired doctor-companion, and in the development of their lives together she is proved to be not too far from right. At any rate, Dick can never settle in his mind which of the two roles he is likely the more to serve. It is only too painfully obvious that she is "using" him, in the manner of a patient's exploiting her doctor's will.

> The dualism in his views of her—that of the husband, that of the psychiatrist—was increasingly paralyzing his faculties. In these six years she had several times carried him over the line with her, disarming him by exciting emotional pity or by a flow of wit, fantastic and disassociated, so that only after the episode did he realize with the consciousness of his own relaxation from tension, that she had succeeded in getting a point against his better judgment.

While Nicole "uses" him (drains him of his energies) so that she might advance her cure, the Warren money (administered by the redoubtable "Baby") gradually triumphs over his struggle for independence. It is not merely a "professional situation" being ruined by deep personal involvement; it is also a destructive circumstance, the harsh, cruel, privileged "rich boy" inevitably crushing out the naïve promise and generous soul of the Fitzgerald hero.

The novel had best be entitled *The Decline and Fall of Doctor Diver.* Diver absorbs Nicole's illness to himself; as she grows well, he weakens. He had been a man of abundant promise; he becomes slowly, painfully, a "ward" of the Warren money and a parody of his former gracious self. "You used to want to create things," Nicole tells him, near the end. "Now you seem to want to smash them up." The conclusion of the marriage is inevitable. Nicole breaks from her patient role of dependence upon her doctor-husband, begins to view him dispassionately, and is shortly in the arms of another, a younger man, to whom she goes as though upon release from a hospital. Entirely cured, she "cut the cord forever. Then she walked weak in the legs and sobbing coolly, toward the household that was hers at last."

The "case was finished." Doctor Diver is "at liberty." Exhausted, he turns to the Riviera beach that has served so much of the time as the scene of the cure.

> "I must go," he said. As he stood up he swayed a little; he did not feel well any more—his blood raced slow. He raised his right hand and with a papal cross he blessed the beach from the high terrace.

There are several ironies involved. Not the least of these involves Diver's giving in to a "professional situation" and sacrificing himself for love's sake to a person who is more patient than loved one. But other ironies inhere in this. Nicole's illness is after all the result of the Warren situation, caused by the blurring of moral lines that its immensity of wealth and privilege had fostered. The wealth continues to plague Diver; he is victimized again and again by it. In the end his energy of personal will cannot cope with it. Most of all, the novel describes the impotence of a secular art of healing in the face of such odds as are evident from the beginning. Diver's colleagues, inured by a better training and a less generously human though a sounder background, believe in limiting human situations to the terms upon which they might be scientifically treated. This Diver cannot do; or he cannot will so to limit himself. Like many another Fitzgerald hero, he wishes somehow to heal the world by means of good will and an ingratiating smile. His fund of moral capital (his "charm," as Fitzgerald most often terms it) is slowly drained, by the demands of those about him, who are weaker than he and therefore dependent upon him. He inherits this moral good will from his father, the great naïve American moral hero. Diver is therefore both more and less than a scientist; he is a man of generous gifts, who tries to use psychiatry as an instrument of his good will. He cannot be satisfied to work within the limits of professional discretion, but must give of his fund of love. Because his instincts are to do more than "treat" Nicole (he would love her as well), he becomes involved with her and is defeated by her as a psychiatric "case" and by the causes that lie behind the illness.

A DOCUMENT OF FITZGERALD'S DECLINING MORALE

This pathetic tale is an indication of Fitzgerald's own state of self-realization at the time. The great change in the text of *Tender Is the Night* in the "Dick Diver" version is matched by other reviews of himself and of the 1920s: in the short story, "Babylon Revisited" and in his public confession (in *Esquire,* December, 1934; March and April, 1936) of his own breakdown. There seems to have been something almost frantic about the writing of *Tender Is the Night*, as though he were taking note of his own excesses in the course of describing those of his creatures. The novel is therefore a document of his own declining morale, his own suffering, above all his terrible fright over the spectacle of his descent. Psychiatry was a part of his experience at the time; it became a part of his explanation of the world of the 1920s as he came then to see it. In so doing, he used his knowledge of psychiatry freely, as a layman would who had somehow to know enough about its functioning to comprehend what was happening to him and to the world in which he had always lived.

Trapped in a Mask

Robert Sklar

Dick Diver faces an insoluble dilemma, points out
Robert Sklar, assistant professor in the University of
Michigan's Program in American Culture. He is
loved because he has assumed the guise of the genteel romantic hero. The conventions of the romantic
hero, Sklar explains, were designed to earn romantic
love and hide sexual desire. When Diver recognizes
his physical desire for Rosemary, the conventions of
the past become unsatisfactory and he wants to remove the mask. However, Rosemary's affection for
him is based on his persona; he risks losing her love
if he expresses his physical desire.

Dick Diver's past is neither the ante-bellum South nor the
frontier West but rather the genteel middle-class America of
the late nineteenth century, the "whole-souled sentimental"
America similar to the German and English and French so-
cieties that went to war in 1914 and blew themselves up
"with a great gust of high explosive love." Dick's past is the
world of "religion and years of plenty and tremendous
sureties and the exact relation that existed between the
classes," the world the war destroyed, as Amory Blaine
learned in *This Side of Paradise,* as Dick Diver mourns.
Dick's past is the world of genteel romantic love, a world of
romantic imagination, where neither love nor imagination
steps outside the bounds of social convention. Dick Diver is
yet one more version of the conventional genteel romantic
hero; but like all of Fitzgerald's genteel heroes he is also
something more—like Gatsby a creative figure, in Dick's case
a re-creative figure, who restores the lost utopia of the past.
"Their own party was overwhelmingly American and sometimes scarcely American at all. It was themselves he gave
back to them, blurred by the compromises of how many
years." He brought the past to life again, the utopian Ameri-

can past, the imaginary American past; as Gatsby believes you really might repeat the past, so Dick believed you really might return to it. But on returning, the past can only be what it was before, the conventional, late-nineteenth-century, genteel America. As a genteel hero, Dick can imagine romantic dreams of love and magic possibilities; as a creator, he can build those dreams into a living world; yet he suffers still as does any genteel hero who sees through or beyond the conventions, and his carnivals of affection that make a new romantic world for others serve for him only as massacres he had seemingly ordered to satisfy an impersonal blood lust.

But his blood lust in fact is not at all impersonal. As the soldiers of World War One had fought and died for love, so too Dick stages his massacres for love, for personal love. Rosemary's love for him brings out his motive through Book One. "'You're the only girl I've seen for a long time,'" Dick says to her back on the beach, "'that actually did look like something blooming.'" She blooms for him, as her name signifies, as a symbol of remembrance, literally as the dew from the sea. She brings to him youthfulness and memories of his own youth—his own equivocal, genteel youth. It is her presence that compels him to give a "really *bad* party," to invite the light-skinned crowd, the climbers and the outcasts, as a way of showing off the virtuosity of his playful imagination. Rosemary has just come to feel that the Villa Diana was the center of the world when to her chagrin the outcasts enter through the gate. "Rosemary had a sharp feeling of disappointment—she looked quickly at Dick, as though to ask an explanation of this incongruous mingling. But there was nothing unusual in his expression. He greeted his new guests with a proud bearing and an obvious deference to their infinite and unknown possibilities. She believed in him so much that presently she accepted the rightness of the McKiskos' presence as if she had expected to meet them all along." It is Rosemary's naïveté and romanticism that eventually overcome the incongruity of the scene, but despite the light touch of irony in these sentences Dick's utopian powers are at work, however incommensurate with their objects. Dick is showing off his cleverness and Rosemary is won over. The violence that follows is violence that Dick had desired—as a consequence of his impersonal blood lust, and as a foretaste of the personal blood lust that drives him. The military analogy holds: genteel romantic love finds its fulfillment, here as in the First World War, in violence and destruction. Dick's dilemma after his "really *bad* party" lies in his effort to turn genteel romantic love into something else.

The party in the Villa Diana is the first skirmish in the love affair between Dick and Rosemary. It develops through their trip to Paris, the visit to the battlefield, their kiss in the taxicab, to the moment when Dick realizes that "the nursery footing upon which Rosemary persistently established it" annoyed him, and that she "had her hand on the lever more authoritatively than he." From that moment on Dick can no longer be the genteel romantic hero; he was "too shaken by the impetus of his newly recognized emotion to resolve things into the pattern of the holiday, so the women, missing something, lapsed into a vague unhappiness." For Dick now explicitly recognizes what the genteel romantic conventions were invented to hide, his sexual desire for Rosemary.

CONSTRAINTS AND EVASIONS

And so the past to which Rosemary returns Dick is the past of the adolescent boy in Victorian America, the genteel hero driven to sexual dreams and fantasies by the constraints and evasions of his society. The Yale boy casually tells Dick of Rosemary's adventures in a Pullman compartment—a scene Fitzgerald borrowed, significantly, from the last of the Basil Duke Lee stories [in his *Afternoon of an Author*]—and "with every detail imagined, with even envy for the pair's community of misfortune in the vestibule, Dick felt a change taking place within him. Only the image of the third person, even a vanished one, entering into his relation with Rosemary was needed to throw him off his balance and send through him waves of pain, misery, desire, desperation." Dick rushes out to Rosemary's studio on the outskirts of Paris.

> Dignified in his fine clothes, with their fine accessories, he was yet swayed and driven as an animal. Dignity could come only with an overthrowing of his past, of the effort of the last six years. He went briskly around the block with the fatuousness of one of Tarkington's adolescents. . . . Dick's necessity of behaving as he did was a projection of some submerged reality: he was compelled to walk there, or stand there, his shirtsleeve fitting his wrist and his coat sleeve encasing his shirtsleeve like a sleeve valve, his collar molded plastically to his neck, his red hair cut exactly, his hand holding his small briefcase like a dandy—just as another man once found it

necessary to stand in front of a church in Ferrara, in sack-cloth and ashes. Dick was paying some tribute to things unforgotten, unshriven, unexpurgated.

As a symbol of remembrance Rosemary recalls Dick to his youth, makes him see how false his present life is. Ironically she sees his present life as a re-creation of the past, of the true, romantic past; but through Dick's eyes we know his created world is a stage world where the actors play their parts only so long as he directs and plays the lead. But if he will not keep up the play, where can he turn for release? One alternative to his stage direction—to the beach umbrella which Rosemary felt shading her even in Paris—is the true present. The true present has its own stage life, the life of the movie studio that Fitzgerald draws in a brilliant paragraph as a scene from a purgatorial underworld; and when its theatrical props are removed, the present is still a purgatory, inhabited paradoxically by the light-skinned people, the McKiskos, Mrs. Abrams, Campion and Dumphry, suffering through their ambitions and desires. Dick's "really *bad* party" already intrudes the present into the created past—both Brady, the movie director, and the light-skinned group are there—and the mixture is one that produces violence Dick can neither direct nor control, in the duel and again in the shooting scene at the railroad station. The house hewn from the frame of Cardinal de Retz's palace, meanwhile, contains "nothing of the past, nor of any present that Rosemary knew," but "seemed rather to enclose the future so that it was an electric-like shock." The future is a stage-set, too, but a monstrous one, a "Frankenstein" world made up of the dissipated and the exploiters, and after their brief encounter with the "terrible" future Rosemary and Dick are thrown into each other's arms, escaping back to their separate romantic pasts. But for Dick the past is after all no more than a *cul de sac*, a return to the "unforgotten, unshriven, unexpurgated" genteel romantic fantasies, to the fatuousness of a Tarkington adolescent and the jealous pain of youthful desire without the exquisite manners and the charm that make him creative, and make him loved. Dick's dilemma is complete, and he knows it: he cannot be satisfied unless he sexually fulfills the love his genteel romantic heroism earns him; he cannot seek sexual gratification without throwing off his genteel romantic mask; yet without the mask he would no longer be so loved. The genteel romantic person-

ality with which he is blessed and cursed provides no satisfaction, except for others. For Dick Diver there is no dimension of time in which he can find release; more significantly
than ever his infatuation with Rosemary takes place in a
"lush midsummer moment outside of time." . . .

A DESTINY OF HIS OWN MAKING

Dick's flaw is in himself: his destiny of his own making. Yet
his flaw is the flaw of a society: his illusions the "illusions of
a nation, the lies of generations of frontier mothers who had
to croon falsely, that there were no wolves outside the cabin
door." The novel comes to an end, in chapter twelve of Book
Three, with a remarkable recapitulation of its genteel romantic themes. Dick goes to take a last look at the beach.
"'This is his place,'" Nicole says to Baby. "'—in a way he discovered it. Old Gausse always says he owes everything to
Dick.'" But the beach no longer belongs to him now: with a
white sun beating down out of a white sky, even nature de-
nies him. Moving up on the terrace, Dick stops with Mary
North. "'I've spent most of my time defending you this summer,'" Mary says, and Dick replies, "'That remark is one of
Doctor Eliot's classics,'" a reference which calls forth the
genteel culture of the Gilded Age.

"'You're all so dull,' he said."

"'But we're all there is!' cried Mary."

"His eyes, for the moment clear as a child's, asked her
sympathy and stealing over him he felt the old necessity of
convincing her that he was the last man in the world and
she was the last woman . . . their glances married suddenly,
bedded, strained together." For one last moment sexual desire and the genteel romantic dreams seem united: but "his
blood raced slow." Dick Diver, the creator of romantic
dreams who briefly built a beach into a faery-land utopia,
stands up to go. "He raised his right hand and with a papal
cross he blessed the beach from the high terrace."

Dick returns to the upper–New York State country from
which he had long ago set out. Nicole liked to think "his career was biding its time, again like Grant's in Galena." Once
more Dick Diver's career is linked with Grant's. But time
does not repeat itself. Dick had had his moment of obscurity,
like Grant in Galena; had become like Grant a great military
commander, giving parties like love battles out of blood lust;
and ended like Grant the President, a soured, ineffectual

front man for immense and selfish wealth. But there were no more love battles to be fought: in the summer of 1929, when Dick Diver took leave of the beach he had created, the Gilded Age had only a few more weeks to run. The genteel middle-class American culture, which Dick Diver expressed in so remarkable a way, had lost its values in the First World War, and it was soon to lose its economic foundations as well. Dick Diver fades away into the mystery of the American heartland, which had borne him up into his destiny. But its blood, too, raced slow.

Tender Is the Night ends thus without the promise of a new beginning, slips quietly back into the unrecoverable past. Into the novel which occupied nine years of his life, Fitzgerald poured a profusion of themes and images, poured all the passion of his social discontent and his historical understanding. *Tender Is the Night* is most of all a novel of emotion, of beautiful and sad and sometimes artistically uncontrolled emotion. Through the carelessness of his publisher it was—and still is—a novel of incongruous and distracting imperfections, misspellings, repetitions, wrong words; but through Fitzgerald's own lack of artistic detachment it is also a novel of imperfect form, a novel whose dramatic structure is continually broken by the author's effort to insert a wider social perspective that he felt he had not fully made clear. It was this flaw in the novel's form that led Fitzgerald to plan a structural revision. But when the revised version was posthumously prepared and published it lost the dramatic energy of the novel without gaining the formal clarity that only a textual revision could have attained.[1]

Yet to recognize the lapses of form in *Tender Is the Night* should not detract from the novel's extraordinary achievements. In a way Fitzgerald fulfilled the ambitions with which he had begun his new novel back in 1925. *The Great Gatsby* had placed him among the leaders of the modern movement in the arts, and yet he had wanted to move beyond, to write a novel that would be "the model for the age that Joyce and Stein are searching for, that Conrad didn't find." With *Tender Is the Night* he did move beyond the modern movement, moved away from universal myths and toward the pathos of history. This novel is a vision in art of an era in American his-

---

1. The revised version was prepared by Malcolm Cowley from "the author's final revisions" and published in F. Scott Fitzgerald, *Three Novels* (Modern Standard Authors edition, New York, 1953).

tory, of the failure of a society and of an individual who embodied its graces and its weaknesses. In *Tender Is the Night* Fitzgerald created a work of fiction rare in American literature, a novel uniting romantic beauty and also historical and social depth; and he proved by his creation that his art, and his identity as an artist, could survive the death of the society which had nurtured and sustained him.

CHRONOLOGY

1896

Francis Scott Key Fitzgerald is born in St. Paul, Minnesota, on September 24.

1898

Edward Fitzgerald's business fails; the family moves to Buffalo, New York, where he takes a job as a salesman.

1900

Zelda Sayre is born in Montgomery, Alabama, on July 24.

1901

Fitzgerald family moves to Syracuse, New York. Annabel Fitzgerald, Scott's only surviving sibling, is born in July in Syracuse.

1903

Fitzgerald family returns to Buffalo.

1908

Edward Fitzgerald loses his job; the family returns to St. Paul. Scott enters St. Paul Academy.

1909

Scott's first appearance in print: "The Mystery of the Raymond Mortgage" (an Edgar Allan Poe–like mystery) published in *St. Paul Academy Now & Then.*

1911

Scott attends Newman boarding school in Hackensack, New Jersey.

1912

Scott's play *The Captured Shadow* is produced by an amateur theater group in St. Paul while he is home for the summer.

1913

Enters Princeton University.

1914

His first play for the Triangle Club, *Fie! Fie! Fi-Fi!*, tours during Christmas vacation; his poor grades prohibit him from traveling with the show. Home for Christmas, he meets Ginevra King and begins a two-year courtship.

1914–18

World War I; the United States enters the war in 1917.

1917

Eighteenth Amendment to the U.S. Constitution makes alcoholic beverages illegal (federal prohibition law goes into effect in 1919). Fitzgerald leaves Princeton and enters the army as a second lieutenant.

1918

March—Completes the first draft of *The Romantic Egoist* and submits it to Scribner's. (It will later be retitled *This Side of Paradise.*) July—Scott and Zelda meet in Montgomery, Alabama. Scribner's declines *The Romantic Egoist*; in October a revised version is also declined. November 11—World War I ends.

1919

Discharged from the army in February. *This Side of Paradise* is accepted by Scribner's in September.

1920

Fitzgerald publishes *This Side of Paradise* and marries Zelda Sayre. Sinclair Lewis publishes *Main Street.* Women are given the right to vote by constitutional amendment. "Red scare" leads to arrest of twenty-seven hundred American Communists.

1921

May/July—Fitzgeralds visit England, France, and Italy. October—Their daughter, Scottie, is born in Minnesota.

1922

Fitzgerald publishes *The Beautiful and Damned.* James Joyce publishes *Ulysses*; T.S. Eliot publishes *The Waste Land.* The Fitzgeralds move to Long Island, New York.

1923

Fitzgerald's play *The Vegetable* fails in Atlantic City. Hitler writes *Mein Kampf.*

1924

The Fitzgeralds leave for Europe in April, visiting Paris and the French Riviera. They move to Rome for the winter.

1925

Fitzgerald publishes *The Great Gatsby*. The family moves to Paris, where they meet Ernest Hemingway, among others.

1926

Ernest Hemingway publishes *The Sun Also Rises*. The Fitzgeralds move to the Riviera. In December, they return to America.

1928

After a brief stint in Hollywood and a year in Delaware, the family visits Europe from April until September, when they return to Delaware.

1929

The Fitzgeralds are in Europe again, having been there over six months when the stock market crashes in America on October 29. William Faulkner publishes *The Sound and the Fury*.

1929–37

Great Depression in the United States, following the stock market crash of 1929.

1930

Zelda suffers her first mental breakdown while in Paris; enters a Swiss clinic for treatment. Scott moves to Switzerland to be near the clinic. Zelda will remain in the clinic for fifteen months, eventually being diagnosed with schizophrenia.

1931

Zelda returns to Montgomery; Scott goes to Hollywood to work for MGM.

1932

Zelda's second breakdown; she enters a clinic in Baltimore for four months.

1933

Eighteenth Amendment repealed (see 1917). President Franklin Roosevelt introduces the "New Deal," programs intended to end the depression.

1934

Fitzgerald publishes *Tender Is the Night*. Zelda's third breakdown; she returns to the Baltimore clinic.

1935

Italy invades Ethiopia. Fitzgerald begins writing "The Crack-Up," a collection of essays discussing his ordeals.

1936–39

Spanish Civil War.

1937

Japan invades China. Fitzgerald, deeply in debt, returns to Hollywood. For the next eighteen months, he receives $1000 to $1500 per week as a screenwriter, although he receives only one screen credit (for his work on *Three Comrades*).

1938

Germany invades Austria. MGM does not renew Scott's contract.

1939

John Steinbeck publishes *The Grapes of Wrath*. Scott takes freelance jobs for various Hollywood studios. He begins work on *The Last Tycoon*.

1939–45

World War II. The United States enters the war in 1941, after the December 7 Japanese attack on Pearl Harbor.

1940

December 20—Fitzgerald dies.

For Further Research

BIOGRAPHIES

Matthew J. Bruccoli, *Some Sort of Epic Grandeur: The Life of F. Scott Fitzgerald.* New York: Harcourt Brace Jovanovich, 1981.

Scott Donaldson, *Fool for Love: A Biography of F. Scott Fitzgerald.* New York: Delta, 1983.

William F. Goldhurst, *F. Scott Fitzgerald and His Contemporaries.* New York: World, 1963.

John J. Koblas, *F. Scott Fitzgerald in Minnesota: His Home and Haunts.* St. Paul: Minnesota Historical Society Press, 1978.

John Aaron Latham, *Crazy Sundays: F. Scott Fitzgerald in Hollywood.* New York: Viking, 1970.

André Le Vot, *F. Scott Fitzgerald: A Biography.* Translated by William Byron. New York: Doubleday, 1983.

Sara Mayfield, *Exiles from Paradise.* New York: Delacorte Press, 1971.

Jeffrey Meyers, *Scott Fitzgerald: A Biography.* New York: HarperCollins, 1994.

Nancy Milford, *Zelda.* New York: Harper & Row, 1970.

Arthur Mizener, *The Far Side of Paradise: A Biography of F. Scott Fitzgerald.* Boston: Houghton Mifflin, 1951.

———, *Scott Fitzgerald and His World.* New York: Putnam, 1972.

David Page and Jack Koblas, *F. Scott Fitzgerald in Minnesota: Toward the Summit.* St. Cloud, MN: North Star Press of St. Cloud, 1996.

Henry Dan Piper, *F. Scott Fitzgerald: A Critical Portrait.* New York: Holt, Rinehart & Winston, 1965.

Francis Kroll Ring, *Against the Current: As I Remember F. Scott Fitzgerald.* San Francisco: Donald S. Ellis, 1985.

Charles E. Shain, *F. Scott Fitzgerald.* University of Minnesota Pamphlets on American Writers, No. 15. Minneapolis: University of Minnesota, 1961. (Also available as Charles E. Shain, "F. Scott Fitzgerald," in William Van O'Connor, ed., *Seven Modern American Novelists: An Introduction.* Minneapolis: University of Minnesota Press, 1964.)

Andrew Turnbull, *Scott Fitzgerald.* New York: Scribner's, 1962.

CRITICISM

Jackson Bryer, *The Critical Reputation of F. Scott Fitzgerald.* Hamden, CT: Shoe String Press, 1967.

John F. Callahan, *The Illusions of a Nation: Myth and History in the Novels of F. Scott Fitzgerald.* Urbana: University of Illinois, 1972.

Robert Cowley and Malcolm Cowley, eds., *Fitzgerald and the Jazz Age.* New York: Scribner's, 1966.

Katie de Koster, *Readings on* The Great Gatsby, San Diego: Greenhaven Press, 1998.

Scott Donaldson, ed., *Critical Essays on F. Scott Fitzgerald's The Great Gatsby.* Boston: G.K. Hall, 1984.

Kenneth Eble, ed., *F. Scott Fitzgerald: A Collection of Criticism.* New York: McGraw-Hill, 1973.

A.E. Elmore, "*The Great Gatsby* as Well Wrought Urn," in Thomas Daniel Young, ed., *Modern American Fiction: Form and Function.* Baton Rouge: Louisiana State University Press, 1989.

Frederick J. Hoffman, ed., *The Great Gatsby: A Study.* New York: Scribner's, 1962.

Alfred Kazin, ed., *F. Scott Fitzgerald: The Man and His Work.* New York: World, 1951.

Marvin J. LaHood, ed., Tender Is the Night: *Essays in Criticism.* Bloomington: Indiana University Press, 1969.

Richard D. Lehan, *F. Scott Fitzgerald and the Craft of Fiction.* Carbondale: Southern Illinois University, 1966.

Ernest H. Lockridge, ed., *Twentieth Century Interpretations of The Great Gatsby: A Collection of Critical Essays.* Englewood Cliffs, NJ: Prentice-Hall, 1968.

Robert Emmet Long, *The Achieving of The Great Gatsby.* Cranbury, NJ: Associated University Presses, 1979.

Arthur Mizener, "F. Scott Fitzgerald: *The Great Gatsby,*" in Wallace Stegner, ed., *The American Novel: From James*

Fenimore Cooper to William Faulkner. New York: Basic Books, 1965.

Sergio Perosa, *The Art of F. Scott Fitzgerald.* Translated by Charles Matz and Sergio Perosa. Ann Arbor: University of Michigan Press, 1965.

Robert Sklar, *F. Scott Fitzgerald: The Last Laocoön.* New York: Oxford University Press, 1967.

Milton Stern, *The Golden Moment: The Novels of F. Scott Fitzgerald.* Urbana: University of Illinois, 1970.

Brian Way, *F. Scott Fitzgerald and the Art of Social Fiction.* New York: St. Martin's Press, 1980.

HISTORICAL OR LITERARY BACKGROUND

Frederick Lewis Allen, *Only Yesterday: An Informal History of the Nineteen-Twenties.* New York: Harper, 1931. Reprint, New York: Perennial Library, 1964.

Ralph K. Andrist, ed., *The American Heritage History of the 20's and 30's.* New York: American Heritage, 1970.

A. Scott Berg, *Max Perkins: Editor of Genius.* New York: E.P. Dutton, 1978.

Matthew J. Bruccoli, *Scott and Ernest: The Authority of Failure and the Authority of Success.* New York: Random House, 1978.

Paul Allen Carter, *The Twenties in America.* New York: Crowell, 1968.

———, *The Uncertain World of Normalcy: The 1920's.* New York: Pitman, 1971.

Malcolm Cowley, *Exile's Return: A Literary Odyssey of the 1920s.* New York: Norton, 1934. Revised and expanded edition, New York: Viking, 1951. Edition with introduction and notes by Donald W. Faulkner, New York: Penguin, 1994.

Lynn Dumenil, *The Modern Temper: American Culture and Society in the 1920s.* New York: Hill and Wang, 1995.

Ellis Wayne Hawley, *The Great War and the Search for a Modern Order: A History of the American People and Their Institutions, 1917–1933.* New York: St. Martin's, 1979.

Ernest Hemingway, *A Moveable Feast.* New York: Scribner's, 1964.

Joan Hoff-Wilson, ed., *The Twenties: The Critical Issues.* Boston: Little, Brown, 1972.

Ethan Mordden, *That Jazz! An Idiosyncratic Social History of the American Twenties.* New York: Putnam, 1978.

Richard Brandon Morris and James Woodress, eds., *Boom and Bust: 1920–1939.* New York: McGraw-Hill, 1976.

Michael E. Parrish, *Anxious Decades: America in Prosperity and Depression, 1920–1941.* New York: Norton, 1992.

Geoffrey Perrett, *America in the Twenties: A History.* New York: Simon & Schuster, 1982.

Milton Plesur, ed., *The 1920's: Problems and Paradoxes.* Boston: Allyn and Bacon, 1969.

Paul Sann, *The Lawless Decade: A Pictorial History of a Great American Transition, from the World War I Armistice and Prohibition to Repeal and the New Deal.* New York: Crown, 1957.

Arthur M. Schlesinger Jr., *The Crisis of the Old Order, 1919–1933.* Boston: Houghton Mifflin, 1957.

Elizabeth Stevenson, *Babbitts and Bohemians: The American 1920s.* New York: Macmillan, 1970.

Edmund Traverso, *The 1920's: Rhetoric and Reality.* Boston: D.C. Heath, 1964.

THE WORLD WIDE WEB

Websites on the internet tend to be ephemeral—here today, "not at this server" tomorrow. At this writing there are several interesting sites dedicated to Fitzgerald's work. One of these seems likely to remain available for some time to come: the Fitzgerald site at the University of South Carolina. USC has become the repository of the collection of eminent Fitzgerald scholar Matthew J. Bruccoli, and the university created an impressive website in anticipation of the one-hundredth anniversary of Fitzgerald's birth in 1996. New additions to the site appear on occasion, often bits of research by students. The USC Fitzgerald Centenary site can be accessed at this URL (internet address):
http://www.sc.edu/fitzgerald/index.html/

For an online look at one of Fitzgerald's earlier works, the complete text of *This Side of Paradise* can be found at Columbia University's Bartleby Library site, at the following URL (other works will probably be added over time):
http://www.columbia.edu/acis/bartleby/fitzgerald/

WORKS BY F. SCOTT FITZGERALD

NOVELS

1920

This Side of Paradise

1922

The Beautiful and Damned

1925

The Great Gatsby

1934

Tender Is the Night (A new edition "With the Author's Final Revisions," ed. by Malcolm Cowley, was published in 1948.)

COLLECTED WORKS

1920

Flappers and Philosophers

1922

Six Tales of the Jazz Age

1926

All the Sad Young Men

1935

Taps at Reveille

PLAYS

1914

Fie! Fie! Fi-Fi! A Musical Comedy in Two Acts Presented by the Princeton University Triangle Club. Plot and Lyrics by F. Scott Fitzgerald.

1915

The Evil Eye. A Musical Comedy in Two Acts Presented by the Princeton University Triangle Club. Lyrics by F. Scott Fitzgerald.

1916

Safety First. A Musical Comedy in Two Acts Presented by the Princeton University Triangle Club. Lyrics by F. Scott Fitzgerald.

1923

The Vegetable, or, From President to Postman

PUBLISHED POSTHUMOUSLY

1941

The Last Tycoon (unfinished), edited with an introduction by Edmund Wilson

1945

The Crack-Up. With Other Uncollected Pieces, Note-Books and Unpublished Letters. Edited by Edmund Wilson.

1951

The Stories of F. Scott Fitzgerald

1957

Afternoon of an Author. A Selection of Uncollected Stories and Essays.

1962

The Pat Hobby Stories

1963

The Letters of F. Scott Fitzgerald, edited by Andrew Turnbull

1965

The Apprentice Fiction of Francis Scott Fitzgerald, 1909–17, edited by John Kuehl

1973

Bits of Paradise (twenty-one stories by F. Scott and Zelda Fitzgerald), edited by Matthew J. Bruccoli

1979

The Price Was High, edited by Matthew J. Bruccoli

1994

F. Scott Fitzgerald: A Life in Letters, edited and annotated by Matthew J. Bruccoli

Index